REVIEWS

"The author had me at the title, but when I jumped in and took a look, it got even better. This is more than a book; it is a collection of important bits of wisdom taken from life experiences and organized to help those who love someone become a more supportive and intimate partner. This "couple's manual" by Dr. Anne Burns Harris would be particularly effective for military couples, who truly know the meaning of the phrase 'stressful life.'"

-Nicholas Warr, Author
Phase Line Green: The Battle for Hue, 1968

"After working with couples for twenty years and using many resources, this book is by far the *best* I have seen on relationships; I will use it in couples counseling. It teaches couples how to navigate away from that temporary anger that comes up—a navigation that leads them back to love."

-Reverend Carol West
Pastor, Celebration Community Church, Fort Worth, Texas

"Thank you, Anne Burns Harris! What a resource! Anne has put her wisdom and what she has learned over thirty years of working with couples into this very accessible workbook. She knows what barriers keep intimate relationships from working and in this book she provides easy to use, simple strategies for overcoming these barriers. Anne does not promise easy or quick solutions, but she does, with great patience, walk couples through a clear process for finding solutions. Reading the book is like sitting in her office (at a fraction of the cost as she points out). I will have copies in my office for my own clients. This is a must-read for committed couples who want to improve their relationship."

-Judith D. West, Licensed Clinical Social Worker,
Brevard, North Carolina

"A well-done, highly-pragmatic program for couples, Dr. Harris' book is a treasure both for clients and therapists. Dr. Harris has developed an incredibly useful and usable system for helping couples become stronger and more intimate as they grow together through life. This is an amazingly user-friendly system to help couples build a strong foundation in their relationship as well as confront conflict in a healthy manner. A carefully crafted work filled with illustrations, personal vignettes and a great deal of wisdom, Dr. Harris' book is a great guide for building a strong foundation in an intimate relationship."

-Barbara Lea, Ph.D.
Clinical Psychologist, Asheville, North Carolina

When Two Souls . . . Find Each Other . . ."
_{BST}

SOMEONE still needs to take out the trash

From every human being there arises a light
That reaches straight to heaven
And **when two souls** that are destined to be together
Find each other,
Their streams of light flow together,
And a single brighter light
Goes forth from their united being.

Baal Shem Tov
Jewish Mystic

"When Two Souls . . . Find Each Other . . ." BST

SOMEONE still needs to take out the trash

Anne Burns Harris, Ph.D.

Grateful Steps
Asheville, North Carolina

Grateful Steps
1091 Hendersonville Road
Asheville, North Carolina 28803

Harris, Anne Burns

Cover Art by Jean Burns Pudlo
Greensboro, North Carolina

"When Two Souls . . . Find Each Other . . ."
SOMEONE *still needs to take out the trash*

A RELATIONSHIP MANUAL FOR COUPLES

ISBN 978-1-935130-08-6 Paperback

Printed by BookMasters
Ashland, Ohio
FIRST EDITION

LIBRARY OF CONGRESS
CATALOGING-IN-PUBLICATION DATA
Harris, Anne Burns.
  "When two souls find each other-- " : someone still needs
to take out the trash : strategies for committed couples /
Anne Burns Harris. -- 1st ed.
p. cm.
  ISBN 978-1-935130-08-6 (pbk. : alk. paper)
  1. Man-woman relationships. 2. Nurturing behavior. 3.
Self-help techniques. I. Title.
HQ801.H328 2009
646.7'8--dc22
                                    2008048349

www.gratefulsteps.com

This book is dedicated to

Bernard B. Harris

BERNIE-my friend, my partner, my lover and my Soul-Mate

To My Teachers

What I have to teach reflects the integration of what I have learned from others during my years training to become a therapist. I want to list the most influential of my teachers. Some taught me in traditional academic settings. Most are therapists themselves—mainly in the field of Gestalt Therapy—who taught me the art of therapy. It is from them that I learned many of the specific techniques I am teaching you in this book. I am deeply grateful to them all for their influence in my life and my work, and I want to pause here and say "Thank you." I hope they will be happy to see their skills and ideas—albeit with my interpretation—passed along to you in this book. I list them in the order in which they entered my life: Sister Eileen Delores, IHM, Jack Mulgrew, Sue Moss, Ernie Andrews, Gertrude Krauss, Isadore Fromm, Joseph Zinker, Erv and Miriam Polster, Jim Simpkin, Edward Smith, Faculty of The Fielding Institute.

I would also like to recognize and thank the people who supervised my work early in my career: Lib Harkins, John Esse, Jack Mulgrew, Barbara Lea.

Acknowledgments

So many wonderful family members, steadfast friends, colleagues and former clients have encouraged me over the past couple of years to bring this book to fruition. I wish to thank everyone who has called, written or spoken words of support during this time. Your confidence in me and in my ability to complete this project is deeply appreciated. Thank you so much!

I specifically want to list by name the people who have actively participated in this process, either by reading or editing early drafts or by providing guidance about publishing. In alphabetical order, they are: Kathy Bowser, Jim Burns, Jim DeLeo, Gina Frey, Daniel Harris, Lynn Harris, Millicent Jones, Betty Mack, Nancy Marlowe, Paul Moran, Judy Nebrig, Jean and Ron Pudlo, Carol Taylor, Alice Wellborn, Judith West. Jim Burns and Nancy Marlowe, in particular, gave hours of their time editing the first complete draft. Their combined efforts led to a well-edited manuscript. Jean Burns Pudlo's generous contribution of her artwork for the cover captured the book's focus perfectly.

A special thanks goes to my husband, Bernie, who patiently read the very first draft and every version since. He has remained constantly encouraging and supportive of my efforts.

I thank all the staff at Grateful Steps, especially Twila Jefferson, for the skill and energy in turning this project into a published book.

Lastly, I thank Pasquale and Christina Guggino, the original Pat and Chris, for the use of their names, their support and their years of friendship.

TABLE OF CONTENTS

INTRODUCTION

"I love you. I'm pissed and I love you." My husband whispered these two short sentences to me as I lay in bed contemplating divorce. They are, perhaps, the most important two sentences he ever said to me. Speaking them allowed us to reconnect in the midst of a very difficult argument. The important reality captured in that moment is that in a solid relationship, anger and love can coexist temporarily. There are solutions that allow the anger to be dealt with and strengthen the love. This book presents strategies for those, as well as strategies for other situations that are part of a committed relationship.

I am dedicated to the preservation of marriage. **By marriage I mean a committed relationship between two people who love, care for and respect one another and who have resolved to create between them an ever developing intimacy and energy which spills over into the lives of the people in their world.** In my personal life, I have lived as a single person, I have experienced communal religious life and I have been married. Each state of life has had its positives and negatives, but I have concluded that the challenges and rewards of intimacy are some of the richest experiences one can have. Intimacy can also create some of the most painful and wrenching experiences one can have. In my professional work I have supported committed relationships and I am writing now to share what I know with you.

It has taken me 1,560 weeks to learn what I have put into this book. That's 30 years. That is how long I have been working as a therapist with couples. **You can learn it in 14 weeks or less.** Fourteen weeks is less than one third of one year. If you value your relationship, reading this book—with your spouse—is a good way to spend the next few months. Through it you can discover how to make changes which can affect your happiness for the rest of your lives. What I have to teach you is a set of clear, specific and simple skills. Together you can learn to use these tools and make them work for you.

In the past thirty years I have seen these techniques work with very angry people, very sad people, very frustrated people and very discouraged people. Couples who have not had sex in over a year have been able to reintroduce intimacy into their lives. Couples who have not been able to complete a sentence with one another without interruption have learned how to listen and how to come up with ideas and solutions to problems which they both agree will change their lives. If you are in a committed relationship and you want "it" to work, read this book.

Three Couples Use This Book

This proves to be a good book for all three. Read about their situations and see if it is the book for you:

Sam and Sandy

There is tension in the air. Things are different. There has been no sex for months now. Communication feels cold and trite. Something has changed. Sam and Sandy work flex schedules which allow them time with each other every morning. They have always talked regularly and they have prided themselves on being able to work out problems. Recently, however, they are having the same fights over and over again and they can't figure out why. There is too much uncomfortable quiet in the house. The old closeness between them seems to have vanished and they both agree there is more sarcasm in their words than either of them can remember. Sam suggests using this book. They already take time for themselves and talk regularly, but the connection is missing. What they need is a set of tools to use to get more clarity and some techniques to help them actually resolve issues rather than discussing the same topics over and over again. They are getting bogged down and missing each other. Now is the time to change!

Judy and David

Judy's dad died last year, and much of her energy of the past few months has been devoted to helping her mother make this difficult transition and get settled in her new apartment. David is completely supportive of this but has had to take over much more of the childcare. He is good at it, and he and his thirteen-year-old son are still getting along, but his two daughters are another matter. At eleven and eight, they are lively and demanding, and David feels they need more time with their mother. He and Judy have no time with each other, and he can sense a tension in the house that he is not used to feeling. He and Judy have finally talked and have agreed to start reading this book and doing the exercises. Since they are in such a stressful period, they agree they need to start at the beginning of the book and make it a priority.

Jean and Jackie

Jackie's tenth high school reunion is this year, and after all this time it might be nice to travel back to the home town. Jean and their son, Brian, could come along for the trip, but it means spending a good deal of time with Jackie's family. In the past visits like that have been very stressful. Jean usually becomes exhausted trying to support Jackie, and both of them object to the "kid style" Jackie's parents have with Brian. They are much more into rules and punishment than either Jean or Jackie has ever been and act more like the parents than the grandparents. After the last visit Jean ended up angry and Jackie was in tears. This time, they want to think through the trip and this big event in advance, and they want some techniques to use with each other to help them stay on topic, speak clearly with one another and make some solid plans. This book will help.

If you met these couples would you have anything in common to share with them? Do their situations remind you at all of your own? If you feel a connection, keep reading.

As you go through you will see some of the ways these couples have become trapped. You'll see that Sam and Sandy have begun to speak in shorthand instead of taking the time to communicate what they really mean. Because everything is related, they move quickly from one topic to another without resolving anything. They are so used to talking with one another that they are unaware they have slipped into a pattern of leaving issues unresolved, building tension between them. Judy and David are both in a period of mourning and yet the demands of life continue for them. In this book you will see how they learned to set aside regular times to talk and regular times together just to recover and have some sense of connection during this difficult period. You will also reflect on some patterns they might want to change with their children. Finally, you will see how Jean and Jackie could put some protective boundaries in place and establish some connecting rituals to help them during the stress of the trip they would like to take together. As you read you will have some ideas to share with all of these couples and we will check in with them from time to time to see how they are doing with the exercises so you can even compare notes. By the end of this book they will have made changes and so will you.

Many have walked this road

Many of you who are reading have been my clients. To you I say, "Here is the book, as promised." To those of you whom I haven't known as clients, you and I owe a debt of gratitude to all those people who over the years trusted me enough to sit in my presence and face the truths about their relationships. As I taught them, they taught me.

In my office, there have been old faces in confusion, young faces in anger, middle aged faces in hurt. Men and women have sat in front of me hoping to salvage something or remake something of their marriages. Gay couples have sat there, too, trying equally hard to piece together a relationship that is falling apart. I have witnessed courage, disgust, frustration, tenderness, roughness and gentleness. The intimate relationship is the most demanding of relationships even as it has the potential to be the most fulfilling.

I see each of you now as if we were together in that office. I am picturing you as present with me here at my computer because it is very different for me to do this in writing rather than face to face. So much of what would evolve in a therapy session would seem to spring spontaneously from whatever interaction was occurring with the couple at that moment. That can happen here, as you read this book and engage in the process. I trust that this book will be helpful to you in your relationships. In it I share with you the ideas and structures that were in my head as I participated in those couples' sessions in my office.

Some couples would come into my office in deep pain. Some were too estranged from each other to really make the effort needed to reconnect. Many came when they noticed that things were just not as good as they had once been or when they feared they were past the point of meaning in terms of being with each other. Every now and then I would have an engaged couple or a couple newly committed to each other who would want some sessions preventatively. They saw some value in establishing patterns early on that might help them. Wherever you find yourselves in your relationship I hope you can flip through this book and find a page which is helpful.

Actually, I really hope someone gave you this book as an engagement present or a present on the day of your commitment ceremony to one another. If you are at that stage of life together you will look at these suggestions and chuckle, because they will seem to be so simple and easy. Now is the time to put them in place in your life.

Most of us, however, don't get around to looking at the manual until we have exhausted every other possibility at fixing something. I was once trying to install software on my computer and I was totally frustrated. My niece offered to help, but when she saw what I was doing, she said, with her seventeen-year-old computer savvy and wisdom, "Aunt Anne, start at the top of the page and *read* what it says to do." My hope is that you will start at the top of the pages in this book and read what it suggests. Try the exercises. Be patient with each other.

What you will find in this book

The book is laid out to guide you step by step through a process intended to change patterns in your relationship. The first step is setting aside the time to devote to yourselves so this can happen. It has always fascinated me that in our society we schedule everything. We have PDAs, calendars on cell phones, planners, desk calendars and prompts on our computers, which we use for every facet of our lives—except our relationships. Somehow we get stuck in the belief that if being together does not happen spontaneously it is not meant to be. If we used that approach to our jobs, shopping, homework or anything else in life, absolutely nothing would get done.

Relationships require a time commitment. When the patterns of relating become stuck they require techniques to get them past the impasse. One of the ways you will use the time you set aside for yourselves will be in learning some of these techniques. Try to remember my niece's advice. *Start with the first step and make sure you know what you are doing with it before you move on to the second step.* Because these techniques are like a scaffolding they look deceptively easy. Theoretically they are simple; but you do not live in a theory. You live a real life. You bring to your relationship individual histories, and you are dealing with current real life issues. What you are trying to do here is not easy. *The skills you will learn are simple, but they require a certain focus and discipline to work.*

You may decide that it is better to read the book alone first and then do the exercises together. It may be better to have two copies of the book so that you can each use your own, underlining and noting what stands out as important from your perspective. This book is intended to be a tool. Use it that way. It is not meant to gather dust on the bookshelf. Fold the pages down. Write in the margins. Make it yours!

I want to say one word of caution about using this book. If you find yourself reading this at a time in life when you are facing a severe crisis, or if you know from your own history that you need professional support when making major changes in your life,

Week 1

then make an appointment with a therapist before you begin any of these exercises.

I especially want to caution couples who have just experienced the death of a child, the diagnosis of a major illness or chronic condition —in any member of the immediate family—or the building of a house together. Over the years I have found that these three situations impact a couple very heavily. If you are thinking you need some changes in your relationship, this would be a good time to work together with a counselor or find a therapist for yourself and bring this book along. Get some support preparing yourself for your part of the dialogues and then go to it!

This is a relationship manual for couples who want it to work. You are going to have to be dedicated to the goal of "making it work" in order to complete this book. The skills are simple but the doing of them is not easy. We are about to embark on a journey together which is demanding. The questions you have to ask yourselves are:

1) Do you really want this relationship you are in to improve, to "work?"

2) Are you willing to commit the time and energy necessary to make that happen?

Some couples will prefer to read this book at their own pace. Others prefer a structure. For those of you who prefer a structure, and for counselors who wish to use this book as an adjunct to counseling sessions, check the Fourteen Week Plan at the end of this section. It may give you a structure for the book which works with your busy schedule. Whatever your style I hope this book proves helpful!

Motivate Yourselves

Part I

Materials needed: phone or computer, phone book, pen or pencil, one envelope

Using your phone or computer find out the following information and fill in the blanks using your pen or pencil:

Sample hourly fee for professional services from a couples' counselor _____

Sample hourly fee for any divorce attorney in your town _____

Pick one of those two numbers and use it to fill in the following sentence on the envelope:

> We saved $_____with this week's hour together!

Even if you choose to use this book with the help of a counselor, which I suggest in various places, the more you can learn to work on your own outside of those sessions the more money you will save.

Part II

Every week when you meet for at least an hour together to work on this book, pay yourselves the amount you would have paid a professional. Just slip the actual cash into the envelope or write yourselves an "I.O.U." and set the money aside in one of your accounts.

Part III

Begin to brainstorm how you are going to use that money to splurge on yourselves! Further directions will be found at the end of this section under the title "WEEK FOURTEEN."

A note to professional counselors or students: This book is based mainly on Gestalt Therapy and Cognitive Behavioral Theory. You will also find Ericksonian techniques, some ideas reminiscent of Neuro-Linguistic theory and Attribution Theory. Overall the book is intended to be more educational than psychotherapeutic and you will see places where I indicate that therapeutic support and intervention would be both helpful and warranted. The Fourteen Week Plan is designed to allow time for new skills to become permanent. The tasks are designed so that more complex skills are introduced after the more basic ones have been practiced sufficiently to achieve success and allow a sense of confidence to develop.

FOURTEEN WEEK PLAN

WEEK ONE
Read the Introduction and the first part of Chapter one. (pp. 1-24)
Stop after completing Rehearsal Meeting #1. (p. 24)

WEEK TWO
Maintain twenty-minute daily contact.
Complete Rehearsal Meeting #2. (p. 25)
Read and complete pages 27-35.

WEEK THREE
Maintain twenty-minute daily contact and schedule a weekly fun break.
Use weekly meeting to complete Chapters Two and Three. (pp. 36-45)

WEEK FOUR
Maintain twenty-minute daily contact and weekly fun breaks. Finish Chapter 1, 2 &3.
Read Chapter Four and complete exercises. These can be the focus of the weekly meeting. (pp. 46-53)

WEEK FIVE
Maintain twenty-minute daily contact and weekly fun breaks.
Study Chapter Five: The Steps of Processing. (pp. 54-60)
Complete #1 in Chapter Six. (pp. 61-62)

WEEK SIX
Maintain twenty-minute daily contact and weekly fun breaks.
Use weekly meeting to complete Scenarios #2, 3 and 4 with Chris and Pat. (pp. 63-68)

WEEK SEVEN
Maintain twenty-minute daily contact and weekly fun breaks.
Use weekly meeting to begin processing your own personal issues. (pp. 69-72)

WEEK EIGHT
Maintain twenty-minute daily contact and weekly fun breaks.
Use your weekly meeting to process personal issues. Consult pages 70-71 as a guide.
Begin reading Chapter Eight on your own. (pp. 73-83)

WEEK NINE
Maintain twenty-minute daily contact and weekly fun breaks.
Finish reading Chapter Eight on your own and use your weekly meeting to process
personal issues. (pp. 83-93)

WEEK TEN
Maintain twenty-minute daily contact and weekly fun breaks.
Use weekly meeting to read Chapter Nine and complete Illustration #1. (pp. 94-111)

WEEK ELEVEN
Maintain twenty-minute daily contact, weekly meeting and weekly fun breaks.
Use weekly meeting to review Chapter Nine and have fun with pages 112-116.

WEEK TWELVE
Maintain twenty-minute daily contact, weekly meeting and weekly fun breaks.
Use your meeting time to complete Chapter Ten (pp. 116-131)

WEEK THIRTEEN
Maintain twenty-minute daily contact and weekly fun breaks. Begin reading Chapter
Eleven on your own (pp. 132-139). Use your weekly meeting to process personal issues
and work your way through any impasses.

WEEK FOURTEEN
Maintain your twenty-minute daily contact. Use your weekly meeting to complete
Chapter 11 including the exercises (pp. 140-152). Take your weekly fun break by reading
Chapter 12 together (pp. 153-156). ***Congratulate yourselves, count the money in your***
motivational envelope, CELEBRATE— and plan to splurge!

1

TIME TO GET STARTED

Welcome to my virtual office! I hope the two of you are reading this together. If I were a betting woman, which I might be if I had any luck at that sort of thing, I would bet that one of you recently said, "We really need to get this book . . . make some changes . . . get ourselves out of this funk we are in"—or some such comment. I would further bet that the other person—perhaps sighing inwardly—reluctantly agreed; and so here you are! That was the scenario I heard most frequently over the last thirty years. Every now and then the decision to come to my office was completely mutual, but that was rare.

It doesn't matter who got the idea first. Perhaps that person is like the canary in the coal mines . . . the first to feel that something is wrong. If so, you both want to respect that person's early warning system. It is one of the many strengths you have in your relationship. No matter how you got to the point of reading this page, I welcome you both and look forward to our working together in ways that I hope you will find helpful. Let me give you some hints about how this book is set up:

- If I am talking generally about ideas or theory or skills, you will see that the typeface font is like this:

   Here is an idea.

- If there is something specific for you to do, I will use italics like this:

   Here is a task.

- If there is an important point I want to stress or if we are in the midst of working through an exercise together and I want to get your attention, the type will change to this:

   Here is an important point.

- ☯ is a symbol which indicates you are about to work with a fictional vignette about a life situation couples face.

Consider this . . .

Anne's Reflections
   From time to time you will see a blocked section. These boxes include sentences I have found myself saying frequently over the years, and I repeat them in this context so that you will hear them, too. The sentence or phrase will be underlined and my reflections on the phrase will be printed in a gray box like this.

Are you ready?

Let's begin! Your participation starts immediately. This is a book "to do," not just a book "to read." What happens between the two of you as you read is the power of the book. You are the ones living your lives. You will know what needs attention. This is a cooperative effort. It is a workbook. You will be asked to do a number of things that may be new to you. I will stay with you as you work your way through these challenges. We are going to start with time.

The first assignment I always gave couples in my office was that they needed to find about four and a half hours a week to spend on themselves. There are 168 hours in a week. Out of that available time they had to find these hours for themselves, and it was not easy. Now it is your turn to find those hours.

I will walk you through what kind of time I'm talking about here and help you think through how to make these hours available for yourselves. The topic of time is at the beginning of this book, because this step is crucial to all the other steps. It is often the hardest, too, so once you have accomplished the task of finding these blocks of time you can have confidence that you can do anything else in this book.

You are going to be looking for three different kinds of time. First you are going to look for twenty minutes a day, probably in the evenings during your work week. (Even though I describe this as twenty minutes a day, most people establish this practice only during the evenings of the work week, typically on Monday, Tuesday, Wednesday and Thursday. They then use the other three days for the remaining blocks of time. For those of you doing the math, it comes to four hours and twenty minutes a week based on this pattern).

After you establish the twenty minute pattern, you are going to look for another three hours: one for a weekly meeting and two for fun. Just for a minute, think of your relationship as a car. The twenty minutes is for maintenance; the one hour is for necessary repairs; and the two hour block is for a joy ride, an excursion, or a Sunday afternoon drive on the Parkway.

Week 1

This is Sam and Sandy's plan:

Sunday	Monday	Tuesday	Wednesday	Thursday	Friday	Saturday
Mtg. 2 p.m.	Daily 20	Daily 20		Daily 20	Daily 20	FUN/p.m.

"Daily" Twenty minutes: Monday, Tuesday, Thursday, Friday
after breakfast (Sandy bikes with friends on Wednesday)
Weekly meeting: Sunday afternoon
Fun time: Saturday night

Twenty Minutes A Day

This is the first step you will take in changing your relationship. Find twenty minutes a day when you can be together, without distractions, to talk with each other.

What is the best time of day to set aside the twenty minutes? That is very individual. After breakfast, before supper, after dinner but before TV are all good choices. Any block of time—other than bedtime—is a good choice. The problem with bedtime is that you will be sleepy. Listening to another person with attentiveness and caring takes energy. You need to be awake and have the energy to spend on this task. The challenge is finding a time and sticking to it.

Spend some time talking about the rhythms of your daily life. When are you most likely to be able to have twenty uninterrupted minutes with one another?

1) Take a minute to think about this and each of you write down what you think the best time of day would be for this. Be as specific as you can:

Person A

_____

_____

Person B

_____

_____

2) Look at the two ideas you have written down and spend five minutes talking about the pros and cons of each suggestion. Write them here if that is helpful.

A

Pros_____

Cons_____

B

Pros_____

Cons_____

*3) Evaluate these two ideas and either pick one of them or come up with a compromise. Make a decision. **All decisions in this book are experiments. That means you will try them for a while and then***

evaluate them and decide whether or not they need to be changed.
Make your first decision and write it below:

> We are going to schedule our twenty minutes a day:
> (circle one)
>
> after breakfast   before dinner   after dinner
> _____(other)

How to Use the Twenty Minutes

Now that you have decided which time period you will set aside, let's talk about how you will use these precious twenty minutes. Remember, this is maintenance time. Maintenance of a car is pretty routine. There are certain tasks that are performed regularly. They are not complicated but they are important. It is the same with your relationship. Some of the most important conversation you can have with one another is regular communication about the very mundane and simple things of life. This is a time to practice speaking in a way that you can be heard—and listening in a way that conveys you have heard.

It is a time to talk about dreams, nightmares, what you had for lunch, the drive home, something you heard on the radio or read in the paper or on your favorite blog. Topics can range from small to large in importance. If it is something you want someone else to know about, this is your chance to talk about it. This is not, however, a time for working out problems, scheduling events or complaining. The purpose of this twenty-minute block of time is for you to talk and to be heard and gradually to feel the sense of connection that comes with that simple process.

The rhythm of this kind of listening is not the same as ping-pong. As soon as you get the "ball" you are not going to hit it back immediately. You are going to allow at least a second for those words you are hearing to penetrate inside of you. It will feel much more like the follow through when hitting a golf ball or even the motion used when catching a basketball. If this kind of conversation is not part of your life already, this is how you can begin to do it:

One person starts talking and speaks for ten minutes while the other person listens; after that the roles switch and the speaker becomes the listener. That's it!

I know on the surface this seems like a very small step but for many couples it is huge to make this happen. The challenges are very real. Careers are demanding. Children are demanding. Houses and yards are demanding. Uncle Sam wants your taxes paid. The orthodontist wants the bill paid. Aunt Jane is turning eighty next month, and your parents want you to help with the party. You have a headache . . . a real one . . . and there are five messages on your cell phone and ten e-mails that demand responses. You will not be attending to any of that. You will be talking and listening to one another.

Because you have been together for a while, you may have patterns of conversation which include interrupting one another. This is pretty common in our society. We are often used to moving fast, thinking fast and talking fast. We are not used to "listening slow." **Here is a trick to use if one of you keeps interrupting:** Pick an object, a lightweight ball is good or a stuffed animal . . . anything light or soft will do. Whoever is talking holds the object. If you do not have that object in your hands it is not your turn to talk. At the end of ten minutes the ball moves into the hands of the new speaker. Use a timer to stick to the ten minutes.

Once you have established the pattern of talking with each other every day in this way and you both have the feeling that you get your chance to talk and you are listened to, then you will know it is time to remove this artificial structure of ten minutes each. At that point, just sit and talk with each other about your day for twenty minutes and drop the rest of the structure.

Weekly Scheduled Meeting

After you have decided on your twenty-minute maintenance time and tried it at least once, it is time to look for the two other blocks of time. The first is a one-hour block of time. This hour is for a business meeting about your relationship. It is the time for any necessary repair work, so you need to find an hour when you will both have energy. The other block of time is at least two hours and is for fun and play.

First let's pick the one-hour meeting time. Middle of the week is good if there is one evening that is quiet and you will both be home. Weekend time is also fine, but if you pick a time on the weekend, understand that this is a work meeting. Whether repair work or preventative work, either kind requires alertness and freedom from interruption.

Later we will talk about how to use the time. Right now your job is to find the time and mark it on your calendar.

Find the time

Depending on your schedules look either for a quiet morning hour, noontime or evening.

1) Is there one day of the week when we routinely have an hour that is predictably free?   YES   NO

2) Is there a time of day that is better for both of us? (If one of you is a morning person and the other is an evening person, you may be looking for a lunch time get together.)_____

3) We have decided to experiment with having a weekly meeting on _____
_____ from _____a.m./p.m. to _____a.m./p.m.

Before we go off looking for that third block of time let's stop here and work a little more on this weekly meeting. Actually, I am going to suggest that you have a first meeting right now. Call it a rehearsal. There will be more structure to it soon but for right now set aside an hour and agree to meet to read through the next section together and to work on the assignments in it. If you can use the hour you have just selected as your routine meeting time, that is great; otherwise, find an hour within the next day or two and use it.

"Rehearsal" Meeting

There are three topics for this first meeting. They are:
    1) Place
    2) Distractions
    3) Memory banks

I will take you through each of the topics, suggest your assignment and give you a place to record your decisions. Your job is to take turns talking about each topic. You've already practiced this in your daily twenty minute conversations. Taking turns listening is very important.

Okay. Here you go. Set your timer to one hour. This is a one-hour meeting. You may or may not finish all of the tasks. If you are not finished, the remaining tasks will be handled next time.

1) Place

Establish the place where you will have your weekly meeting. Determine where this will be—whether inside the house or outside of it. Find a spot which is comfortable enough but not where you usually sit around. Hopefully, this will not have to be the bedroom. A bedroom is for sleeping and for sex, not for talking through problems. (If a bedroom is your only available private space, do not sit on the bed. Bring in two folding chairs if you have to.) A kitchen or dining room table may work well—or two chairs in the den. Sofas usually don't work because you want to be able to see each other easily. Recliner chairs are usually too comfortable and leave you at too far a distance from one another. You want to look for a place where you can see each other when you talk and be fairly comfortable but not totally relaxed.

a) List the possible places where you can realistically meet for one hour by yourselves.

_____

_____

_____

_____

b) If either of you has a preference about one of the places listed above say what that preference is and why you prefer it.

c) If you have two different ideas, list the "pros" and "cons" as you did in the earlier exercise:

PLACE A_____

Pros_____

Cons_____

PLACE B_____

Pros_____

Cons_____

d) Make a decision:

Pick a place.
Remember: all decisions are experiments!

> *We will experiment with meeting weekly in this room _____. We've selected these chairs _____ _____.*

2) Distractions

Talk through the kinds of things which would distract either of you during this time together. Typical distractions which have to be controlled for are the TV, phone calls, computer and children. List what these things are and figure out how to handle them.

Phones

Let me take a minute to talk about phones. In my experience, phone Week 1 *calls are the single worst distractor. Alexander Graham Bell did not come down from the "Mountain" with an eleventh commandment when he invented the phone, and yet many of us live our lives as if "Thou shalt not ignore the ring" is the most important commandment in our lives. Land lines are difficult to ignore at home. Call waiting and call forwarding have made us reachable most of the time, and any call coming in on a cell phone is treated with incredible importance. This seems further exacerbated by the practice of making cell phones somewhat like additional appendages on the body. They are so accessible, so persistent, and often the rings are either beguiling or startling. TURN OFF THE PHONE—all of them. This does not mean put the phone on vibrate. It does not mean texting is okay either. Turn them all off. THIS IS TIME FOR THE TWO OF YOU. Period.*

Make a list of potential distractions and how you will prevent them from interrupting you:

Distraction_____
Solution_____

Distraction_____
Solution_____

Distraction_____
Solution_____

(Use extra paper if needed, but address each and every one.)

3) Memory Banks

Set up a system to remember what decisions you've made at your weekly meetings. Do you want to keep notes or a diary, or do you absolutely hate that technique? Do you want to make funny signs and put them on the refrigerator or on the top of the mirror in the bathroom so you can see them regularly? Do you have exceptional memories and usually agree on what has been decided when you are together?

> We are going to be able to remember decisions we
> made by:
> _____

Remember: all decisions are experiments!

SURPRISE LAST TOPIC FOR YOUR REHEARSAL MEETING:
Take a few minutes and review how you have done so far. You have set aside twenty minutes a day for conversation and that has been happening. You have found an hour a week to use for a business meeting to address issues in your relationship. You have picked a place to have that meeting—and, in fact, you have had your first meeting. Step back and look at how well you have done. Take credit. List some of what you have accomplished:

_____

CONGRATULATE YOURSELVES!
Now, take a break. If you want to read ahead and see the focus of the next section, that is fine; but outside of that put this book down and pick it up again next week at your meeting time. It can be just as damaging to talk too much about your relationship as to talk too little. Follow through on your twenty minutes a day. Put the meeting time on your calendar—all of your calendars—wall, desk, computer, PDA. Put this book where you can find it next week.

Rehearsal Meeting #2

Your first rehearsal meeting was focused on establishing the structure within which you will gradually create a sense of safety for dealing with sometimes difficult, complex or painful issues. You have picked a place and a time. You have taken turns discussing the assigned tasks and you have made decisions.

Week 2

Rounding out our discussion of time, the task of this meeting is to find a two-hour block of time that you can set aside for fun or play every week and to make some decisions about how you might use that time.

Recall the last time you both remember being together without others around and really enjoying yourselves. It may have been last night. It may have been five years ago. The time frame is not important. What you are looking for here is the positive memory. It is also not important if the memory is of some fantastic trip you shared or a moment of shared delight in the accomplishments of one of your kids.

The last time we both remember being together without others around that was fun was:

_____

_____

Tell each other what you remember best about that time. Let yourselves relive one of the good times through memory and by talking about that memory together. Where were you? What do you recall about what happened?

_____

_____

How do you feel as you remember that event, that moment in time? Is there a surge of happiness? Contentment? Sadness as you realize it was so long ago?

_____

_____

The particular feeling is not something to pursue right now. **Just notice that you have feelings and that the feelings are evoked by the memory.**

Next, let's do a sort of brainstorming about the kinds of things you find to be fun. Look at the list below. It is a starting point. Each of you list and check anything that strikes you as fun. You can do two individual versions and compare or agree as you go and check only the ones you both agree on. Adapt it. Make it yours.

☐ Being active	☐ Being active
☐ Watching movies	☐ Watching movies
☐ Eating out	☐ Eating out
☐ Sitting quietly	☐ Sitting quietly
☐ Holding hands	☐ Holding hands
☐ Going to a ball game	☐ Going to a ball game
☐ Hiking	☐ Hiking
☐ Planning vacations	☐ Planning vacations
☐ Going on vacations	☐ Going on vacations
☐ Running errands together	☐ Running errands together
☐ Being in a warm climate	☐ Being in a warm climate
☐ Being in a cold climate	☐ Being in a cold climate
☐ Dressing up	☐ Dressing up
☐ Having sex	☐ Having sex
☐ Going casual	☐ Going casual
☐ Planning in advance	☐ Planning in advance
☐ Doing something spontaneously	☐ Doing something spontaneously
☐ Surprises	☐ Surprises
☐ Other:	☐ Other:

Now you have some ideas for how you might spend "fun" time together. Depending on how things are going for you, "fun" and "play" may mean intimate talking and sex, or it may mean a movie or a DVD. It could mean a tennis game, a cup of tea or a glass of wine shared together on the deck, bowling or a walk in the neighborhood (but not an "exercise" walk—a leisurely conversational walk). It is not important how you define play as long as it is something you both agree would be fun and as long as it is something the two of you do alone together. This is not time to get together with friends or with children. This time is just for the two of you.

I don't want to leave this section without a comment about sex. If you are reading this book, you are in an intimate relationship. If you are in an intimate relationship then sex is probably part of it. If sex is not part of it because of a mutual decision, that is fine; but if sex is not part of your lives on a regular basis because of problems or difficulties between you, that is different. Even while being respectful of these issues and honoring their importance, try to figure out how to put some physical closeness back into the rhythm of your lives. In an intimate relationship, sex is not a luxury. It is the glue which makes a lot of the rest of life easier to endure and handle. I will say more about sex later in the book. But even at this early stage of working on improving your lives together, include as much intimate touch as possible in your fun times together. It is important!

Okay. Now find the time for all of this fun:

Pull out those calendars and look again at the rhythms of your lives. Look for at least a two-hour block of time when you can be without responsibilities and without others around. Put a large X on that two-hour block of time when you find it and label it "OURS." Go ahead for a few weeks and block off the same section from each week. You know the truth of life. If you do not block it off now, by the time you look at it again, someone else's name or project or meeting will be written in that place. This time is going to become sacred to the two of you and will not be given away without mutual agreement that something is important enough to change the date you have with each other.

If your schedules absolutely do not allow two hours once a week, look for a minimum of three hours twice a month. Settle on that only after you've exhausted every attempt at finding a weekly block of time.

As you work on trying to change your relationship to make it richer and happier, it is important to have these "break times" of pure fun. Such moments will help you remember why you chose to be with each other in the first place!

We will come back to other issues about time later in the book, but for now you have taken important steps to be in charge of your "couple time." If you have been able to do some but not all of these steps, keep working at it and see what is possible. Be creative. Be disciplined. Choose yourselves as the priority whenever possible. It is time to do that!

How the three couples handled this first chapter:

Sam and Sandy
. . . had no problem with the daily conversation with one another and worked on details for the weekly meeting pretty easily. But then it came to considering the ideas for how to spend their "fun" time, and they found this

more challenging because they were both missing the intimate sexual time they had been used to having and didn't want to use that time just watching a movie. They decided they were not ready for sex yet but agreed that they were ready to be more intimate than they had been lately. This is what they chose as their "fun" project:

The first week they took a "field trip" downtown and bought massage oil. They smelled all the scents and picked two they liked the best. After this they stopped for an ice cream cone and walked around town for a while window shopping. The second week they used the massage oil and gave each other foot massages.

Judy and David

. . . decided they were not ready for intimacy. They were not even sure they were ready to spend time alone together so they came up with a two-step approach also.

The first week's fun time was spent watching the most hilarious comedy they could find. They made popcorn and invited the retired couple next door over to join them. After a very delightful evening, they realized they could have seen that movie and enjoyed it just as much without company, and so that's what they planned to do the second week.

Jean and Jackie

. . . spent a lot of time working out the details of these first steps with one another. They began talking with each other twenty minutes a day but realized that Jackie's cell phone was a real problem. Jackie's work place was always trying to get in touch, and it took some resolve to turn the phone off. The second challenge they had was finding space in their small house for the weekly meeting, without excluding Brian from his home. Since it was summer time they took advantage of the lawn chairs on the back patio and found they could sit there and talk privately while Brian did his homework and practiced guitar. It wasn't perfect because there were occasional interruptions from him, but it was a good beginning. Finding fun things to do with one another was the easiest thing for them. They quickly made plans and put aside that time.

Consider this . . .

Anne's Reflections
A peaceful relationship is not placid. Peace has rhythms and cycles. There are times of intense action and times of waiting. There is change. There is sameness. Communication flows in an open way no matter what is going on and there is a sense of connection even when living through turbulent times. It is the open flow of energy, thought, action, feelings and words that characterizes peace in a relationship.

2

STRENGTHS AND SKILLS

Y ou have worked hard to put a time structure in place in your lives. As you read through this book, maintain your twenty-minute daily talks and your scheduled two-hour time for fun each week. For now, use your weekly meeting time to read the following chapters together and do the suggested exercises. In this way, as you learn more skills you will also be establishing the pattern of talking regularly about your relationship. In some chapters you will be practicing new techniques while you work on problems other couples have had. Other pages will suggest you focus on your own issues. Whatever the content of the chapter, use your weekly meeting time to work on it together.

This chapter gets you started by asking you to use the time to get a clearer picture of the strengths of your relationship and your individual communication styles. Once you do that, there are some skills I want you to learn or remember. These will be important as we move more deeply into working with content and process in the next chapters. Set your timer for one hour and begin your weekly meeting!

This is the second preparatory chapter, getting you ready for the main messages of the book, which begin in the next chapter. Before you get into learning how to "process" things, there are some skills I want you to learn or remember, and I want you to take a little time to get clarity on the strengths of your relationship and on your individual communication styles. Those are the things that we cover in this chapter.

Strengths

First, let's take time to look at some of your strengths. This section is to help both of you to remember some of the history of survival and accomplishments you've experienced as a couple.

During difficult times or times of change, it frequently happens that the focus turns completely to what is wrong or what needs to be fixed. Suddenly the negative is full screen. The years you have spent together as a couple and how you managed to live those years with each other until now somehow fade from view. Even as you admit that change is necessary, it is very important to take a few minutes to consider ways in which your relationship has thrived in the past.

Oftentimes, partners have done the tasks of partnering well even though they may be hurting in terms of intimacy and closeness. Couples build houses together, establish businesses together, raise children and make parental decisions without rancor, run in marathons together, keep house together and otherwise act as contributing citizens in their communities. Some couples are excellent friends to others and are kind to their respective families.

Before starting to change things in your relationship, take some time to review the base upon which it is grounded. Your relationship is so real that it can be described as a separate "person"—a separate entity from either member of the couple. This relationship has its own life, its own history, its own strengths and weaknesses. When you are looking at the positives you are focusing on its strengths. One area to look at to get an idea of your relationship's strengths is decisions you have made together in the past. Let's start there and see what can be learned from reviewing how you made those decisions.

1) Identify decisions you have made together:
Each of you think of one decision you have made together that you feel good about and tell the other what it is.

2) Recall a time when you were in complete agreement about something:
Take turns. Mention only one time. These "agreements" do not have to be about big life events. They could be as simple as selecting a restaurant you both like, a recreation you both enjoy or a school you both agree on for the children.

3) Identify the strengths you have in the area of decision making:
Examine the decisions you just discussed and the areas about which you have agreement. Begin to look also at how you make decisions as a couple. What patterns do you notice? Who has the ideas? Who makes things happen? Who initiates discussion?

List some of the patterns you see in your decision making:

_____

_____

Here's another positive to consider: Does your relationship have the attributes of flexibility and resilience?

1) Recall one difficult time you have lived through as a couple. Remember how it began, how you handled it and how life changed afterwards. Take turns. Each of you can mention one. Tell the stories to each other. Remember. Take at least ten minutes to do this.

2) Think of one challenge or difficulty each of you has had to face individually. How has the relationship supported and sustained you during that time? What did you ask of the relationship? What did the strength of your relationship provide for you? Use another ten minutes for this discussion.

List what you have noted:

_____

_____

_____

*Look back at the two lists above and name some specific strengths of **your** relationship:*_____

_____

_____

_____

_____

Think back over the conversation of the last few minutes and begin to notice your styles of communicating. Often one person speaks in "broad strokes" almost like painting a canvas with a large brush and many different colors, while the other one speaks in exacting detail similar to choosing the exact stones needed for a flagstone walkway and positioning each one correctly before carefully placing them on the ground. How would you describe your styles?

Speed is another aspect of speech style. Pay attention to speed. Do you speak quickly using many words? Do you speak slowly and deliberately with fewer words? What are your separate styles of communicating? How do you differ in style?

Talk about this together and describe one another's styles. Sometimes, in the midst of intense discussion or high stress situations, we can get so annoyed with the other person that it almost becomes a moral issue how they happen to speak their thoughts. If you can get clarity about your different styles now, in a calm time, it will help you in two ways later on.

The first way it helps is that this understanding will make it less likely that you will sound accusing and angry even when you are frustrated. The second is that once you understand one another's styles, you have taken the first step to learning how to speak in a way that you know will be more clearly heard. I call this "translating."

Think back on the conversation today or reflect on other conversations. Take a minute and say what you think your own style is and then ask for your partner's description of your style. We would describe our styles in these words:

Person A

_____

_____

Person B

_____

_____

Consider
this . . .

Anne's Reflections

<u>Listen with soft eyes.</u> In our society we have been taught to look hard at things, often with critical or pragmatic eyes. Try this experiment: Look at each other. Now, close your eyes and "scrunch" them tightly. Open them slowly and allow yourselves to see one another in this different way. Let yourselves experience the difference. Allow yourselves to simply look softly. This is what I mean by having soft eyes. When listening to one another throughout the exercises in this book, use this as a metaphor and listen with "soft ears." Allow what you hear to enter into you. Look with soft eyes and listen with soft ears, too. Let yourself hear what is really being said instead of letting that hard, critical, pragmatic mind society has trained you to have, get in the way. Soft eyes. Soft ears. Listen.

Skills

The two skills I want you to be familiar with before going further are "I statements" and what I call the "cookie jar phenomenon."

"I" statements are sentences about feelings which begin with the word "I" instead of the usual "you." The word "I" is always followed immediately by a feeling:

◊ I feel hurt . . .
◊ I am angry . . .
◊ I feel very frustrated . . .

In our society we learn a lot of "you" sentences in our homes and schools, not to mention the workplace:

◊ You need to get that to me by 3 p.m.
◊ You must be home immediately after school.

In intimate conversation there is a real value in avoiding the word "you" because it creates an automatic barrier in the flow of conversation. Contrast "You really messed up last night," with "I was really frustrated last night." Say the sentences out loud to one another and see if you can feel the wall coming up with the first one. Practice "I" statements with each other if this is a new concept to you, and keep this technique in mind as you move through the sessions in this book.

Change the following statements to "I" statements. I have provided lines for writing the "I" statement version but you don't have to write them. In fact, there is a real value in hearing the two sentences out loud so you get used to feeling the difference. Do whichever feels easier for you.

1) You are so lazy.
Sample: I get really annoyed when I see you sitting there while I carry this third load of laundry downstairs. I'd like some help.

_____
_____

2) Enough already. You are driving me crazy.

_____
_____

3) It's your mother again. That is the third time this week. You'd think she could find something else to do with her time than call you.

_____
_____

The cookie jar phenomenon has to do with asking questions. You may be surprised to learn that you can make your communication much more powerful and clear if you state your feelings, concerns and requests as a sentence rather than asking questions. Sometimes questions can feel like a trap. I call this the "cookie jar phenomenon." I did not originate this phrase, and it has been so long since I first heard it that I simply can't tell you who might have coined it. This is how it works. Remember back to your childhood. Did you ever hear, "Are you in that cookie jar, again?" or some question like that in your household? This is a scene played out in many ways in the daily comic strips. The response is to freeze, feel guilt or shame and try to get out of answering directly, right? That pattern seems to repeat itself inside us even as adults and has been generalized well beyond the cookie jar situation, making us more sensitive to any question that might be accusatory. Read some of these out loud and see how they sound:

> "Did you like the meal?"
> "How do you like that Harris family?"
> "Do you want to watch TV again tonight?"
> "Have you seen the change I had in that drawer?"

Neutral enough questions—or not. How do you feel when you hear them? Read them again and see how they sound this time:

> "Did you *like* the meal?"
> "How do *you* like that Harris family?"
> "Do you want to watch TV *again* tonight?"
> "Have you seen the *change* I had in that drawer?"

You could ask a question, "Did you park the car in the garage last night?" Right away I begin to suspect I did something wrong. Even if you go on to expand on this question, the feeling is still there. It makes a difference in how I hear the next part: "I had trouble getting the kids and their school packs into it this morning because you left me little room to open the door." Pay attention to how your body responds to these questions. Does your gut tighten a little bit? Does your jaw close? Do you stop breathing? Ask each other the question. See if you feel a certain apprehension or hesitancy before you respond. That is the wall of defensiveness you are going to try to avoid by making statements instead of asking questions. Compare how that question feels to the following statement: "I noticed that you parked the car close to the door of the garage last night. It is a little too close when I'm trying to get the kids and their school packs into it early in the morning. I'd appreciate it if you'd leave a little extra space in the future."

Try some of these. Ask each other the question out loud. See how you feel. Then, read the statement out loud. See if you feel a difference. Maybe you both will. Maybe only one of you will. Maybe this is a non-issue for both of you; but pay attention to your gut's reaction, not your head's.

"Are you ready yet?"
"How many of those do you plan to bring along?"
"Are you playing golf again?"
"Is there another sale on today?"

vs.

"I'm all set to go. Are you ready yet?"
"The car is pretty full. I'm not sure we can fit all of those in."
"I would really like you to be home on Saturday. Could you make that happen?"
"I feel tense when I see you reach for the car keys and your wallet.

Money is tight this week. I'd like to talk about that before you go over to the sale. Would you be willing to do that?"

As we move forward into the next few chapters, remember what you have reflected on in this one. You have reminded yourselves about the strengths of your relationship. You've begun to get a sense of each of your individual styles of communicating and to name them. You have practiced using "I statements" and have become more sensitive to the "cookie jar phenomenon." You will be referring back to all of this when you get into the later chapters in the book.

Rituals

Before going on to the next chapter pause and list at least two daily rituals you are willing to put into your lives. Even as you begin to change your patterns of talking and relating, it is valuable to put some ritual touch and contact into your daily schedules. These might be hugging or kissing as you leave for work for the day or before you go to bed at night. Pick just two and list them here:

1)_____ 2)_____

3

CONTENT

A bar of soap. That's how it began. The first major fight between my husband, Bernie, and me was about the size of the bar of soap in the bathroom. This was the *content* of the fight. In the Introduction you first learned the concepts of *content* and *process*. I want to talk about both of these in more detail here.

Usually, a couple entering my therapy office to talk about their relationship come in focused on content. On the surface content always seems to be the impetus leading to the decision to make changes in a relationship.

Examples of content might be:

"He had an affair."

"She spends all of her time with the kids."

"His parents want to control our lives."

"Her father wants to give us money for a new house."

"He says he'll 'help' around the house but then doesn't follow through."

"She says she cares about my health and my heart condition but cooks fried steak."

List several content areas you are aware of in your relationships

1)_____

2)_____

3)_____

4)_____

5)_____

Week 3

Did you happen to list "soap" as one of your content areas? I'm guessing that you did not; however, to give you an idea of the range of possibilities for content I'll tell you more about that bar of soap. Content topics often seem small, as if they should be inconsequential. For my husband and me the bar of soap only looked small on the surface. Here is some of the background:

I always used a bar of soap until it was melted down to a tiny size and then I'd put that tiny piece on top of the next bar of soap so I used every piece of it. My mother taught me to do this, and my time in the convent had reinforced the practice because we were each given only one bar of soap to last a month. Furthermore, I had been working in a low paying job at the mental health center and had been trying to live within a tight budget. I could save a few cents by having only one bar of soap in the bathroom.

Bernie had always used a large bar of soap. When showering he found it inconvenient to move the bar of soap from the sink to the shower, and when he used my small soap in the shower, it would slip through his hands and fall to the floor. He wanted me to buy larger bars of soap. His hands were larger than mine and while he could hold the large bar quite comfortably, I could not.

(After this issue was resolved, we told a number of friends about it and it became quite a joke. For years when we'd travel and visit a friend's house they'd put out one tiny bar of soap and one *huge* bar.

At the time, however, it was not funny. We became seriously angry with one another over this issue.)

Read over my description of our situation again and see if you can identify some of the areas of content in addition to that actual bar of soap and list them here:

1)_____

2)_____

3)_____

Here are several that I notice as I look back on that incident:

△ Bernie was telling me how things should be done.
△ I was following my mother's example and lesson.
△ I was doing the buying of the soap and felt righteous about my self-discipline.
△ Both of us had taken comfortable and mindless showers for years in our separate bathrooms, and now we were sharing the same one.

You may have found different issues. **Everything is related** and so any content area is a good starting point.

What were some of the real issues here? They had to do with the adjustment to sharing a space and situation that we had handled quite competently, though differently, on our own. So there were adjustment issues. There were independence/dependence issues regarding whose way would prevail about the soap, as well as how much freedom we would give one another in this new way of life together. Family history entered into it in terms of how strongly my mother's messages had been conveyed to me as a child.

In addition to the issues I listed in the paragraph above, I was also hurt and angry at the way Bernie criticized me for the size of the soap; and he was frustrated that I was making such a big deal out of it all. Recognizing these two sets of feelings, switches our focus from content to process. The thoughts and feelings themselves are the content. Process has to do with the *flow* of communication when thoughts and feelings are expressed.

"It's not what you say, it's how you say it"—ever hear that as a child? I want to take this a step further and say that the "how" isn't all that important either. Certainly, there are ways of expressing emotion that make you more easily heard. Paying attention to "I" statements and avoiding the "cookie jar" phenomenon are two of those. They have to do directly with the "how" of communicating. The point I want to make here is that neither the "what" nor the "how" is the most important thing. The most important predictor of good communication in an intimate relationship is being able to say what you have to say in a way that is heard—leaving you with the feeling of having been heard. This happens when the process is open and clear. The process is open and clear when what is stated by one person is heard clearly by the other and responded to in a way that is heard clearly by the first person. The first steps are to identify the barriers that prevent this clarity and to learn how to move around them.

Consider this . . .

Anne's Reflections
<u>Be gentle with one another.</u> A simple practice that is not easy is the act of being gentle with one another. When I would ask couples to be gentle with each other it was usually during a time of incredible stress when emotions were high and when each of them was dangling by their last thread . Making major

changes can produce stress. The self-absorption which results from deep pain, however, leads to an isolation in which each is totally oblivious to the other's struggle. It is not a time when either side can truly hear the other yet; but each one can at least make an assumption that things are difficult and can be gentle rather than harsh. When couples are experiencing intense pain, a certain level of safety has to be achieved before they can talk with each other about what's going on. If you do not feel that safety with each other, it's time to get professional support. I think that safety is best reached in the office of a competent couples counselor. If you are at that kind of place, I would urge you to call and make an appointment. This is not the time to be using this book independently. Get professional help.

Week 3

4

PROCESS

The most amazing example of the power of process that I ever experienced was at a luncheon with my mother in an assisted living facility. At that point she was moving rapidly into the mid stages of dementia. I was visiting her for the weekend and so I joined her at lunch with two of her friends, each of whom also had some dementia. The conversation was animated. There was laughter. There was even some teasing. Everyone talked about what they had done that morning and the plans they had for the afternoon. It was a delightful time and not one bit of content was based in reality! I knew for certain that the things my mother said she had done had not happened, and I was fairly sure that was also true of the other two women. I was aware that what they thought was happening in the afternoon was not at all what was on the schedule. Fortunately, I kept my own sense of reality to myself, and we all had a wonderful time together, but it was the process of talking and being listened to, being accepted and paid attention to, that made that meal a high point of the day. It certainly had nothing to do with the content of the conversation.

"It's not what you say, it's how you say it." How many times that same woman, my mother, in her more youthful self told me that! She meant it in terms of rules of politeness and not at all in the way I'm using it here. What I want to emphasize is that it is not even "how you say it." It is the open flow of the dialogue—the process, not the content. It is the process of the interaction between people that is important. If that process is clear, flowing and open, then any topic at all can be addressed.

If there are walls and barricades, if no one is really listening, if there is not a timely response, if opinions and feelings are ignored or belittled, if any of these block the process—it does not make any difference what the content is. It will not be heard. It is not what you say. It is the ability to say it, be heard, be responded to, and respond. It is the process.

Let's look at that bar of soap again from the perspective of watching the process between my husband, Bernie, and me. As I remember it, Bernie had taken a shower and been thoroughly frustrated with the tiny piece of soap. He sarcastically made some comment about it to me. I was already hurt about something that had happened between us earlier in the day and his sarcasm triggered an equally sarcastic response from me. My sarcasm was sharper than his, so he then became both hurt and frustrated and was getting confused about why this was all such a big deal.

In retrospect we both view this event as pivotal in our relationship, since it occurred early in our lives and forced us to deal with many issues to get through it. We were obviously not talking about soap. We eventually worked that out creatively by buying large bars, which were cheaper, and when they started to get smaller, I would use them and he'd start on a new one! More importantly for us as a couple, this incident focused the spotlight on the way we were communicating (or not!) with one another and how we each got stuck in that process. Let's look a little into that day through this different lens.

Week 4

I had been hurt about something Bernie had done earlier in the day but had not said anything about it. That feeling was simmering inside me. I had to learn to speak my feelings clearly and sooner. Bernie had been sarcastic because at that time in his life he did not yet realize that he got angry. He thought of himself as a kind, mild person. Sarcasm had always been a safe way for him to express his negative feelings indirectly and, he thought, lightly. But sarcasm is a cloak for a dagger. I was raised in a family where sarcasm was used often, and I had well-honed skills for responding to it.

A week or so after this event we actually made a pact with one another that we would not allow sarcasm in our relationship. We have stuck to that deal and whenever either of us has violated this "rule" we made for ourselves, the other has been quick to point it out. Not allowing sarcasm between us was a good rule. We are both too good at being sarcastic, and it would have masked other issues that needed to be worked out.

If the process of our communication had been smoother, the conversation about the bar of soap could have been very simple:

Bernie: Every time I shower using that tiny bar of soap, it slips out of my hand and falls. I have to retrieve it, and I'm afraid I might slip on it. I really want us to get larger bars.

Anne: I can't use the larger bars of soap because they are too big for my hand, but I don't want you to slip in the shower. I hate to spend the money to buy two different kinds of soap because things are tight right now.

Bernie: Why don't we buy the large size, which is cheaper anyway, and I'll use it until it's small enough for you; then I'll get out a new large one for myself.

Anne: Good idea. I'll put it on the shopping list.

Looking at the dialogue, notice that Bernie starts off speaking clearly, stating his issue, explaining why it is an issue for him and asking for what he wants. Anne lets him know she agrees with the concern about his safety. At the same time she mentions the issues that concern her (too large a bar and the cost of it). Considering these issues, Bernie comes up with an idea (brainstorming) and they agree on it. Their words flow freely, unimpeded by barriers. In the initial dialogue, sarcasm had been a barrier. Without it, the process is smooth and clear and open.

Week 4

Sarcasm is one of the red flags to me when I am listening to a couple talk with each other. It is an indirect form of expressing anger which often develops in a family that is not comfortable with the direct expression of anger. Sarcasm thrives in such a situation because it appears to be a "safe" way to get the emotion out. There is always the escape of saying, "I was just making a joke." I like and value satire, and I enjoy a conversation punctuated by quick wit; but sarcasm in intimate relationships is very destructive. It forms a wall that stops the flow of communication. The persons hearing the sarcastic words often feel the sting before they've finished processing the words. Then the actual words spoken send a conflicting message. On the surface, the words sound benign or funny but the sting within them feels threatening and angry. The listener doesn't know which message to respond to and is usually left feeling confused or hurt. This can lead to an **impasse** in the conversation.

An impasse is a place of "stuckness." When people are stuck in an impasse, they feel blocked and cannot figure out how to go on. Chapter Nine explains impasses and presents a variety of techniques for moving past or through them. In that chapter you will learn how to find the 1% solution. Chapter Nine is the most important chapter in this book, but there is a little more ground work to cover before getting to impasses. First, let's review content and process.

In this book there will be many "vignettes" or stories for you to read. In some cases you will be asked to figure out what is going on with a particular couple. Often you will be asked to help solve their problems.

Let me introduce you to Chris and Pat. They are the two people in most of the stories. The stories are all fictional (unless they come from my personal relationship) and they are written in such a way that you get to decide whether Chris is a man or a woman and the same for Pat. So Chris might be Christine or Christopher. Pat might be Patrick or Patricia. It is up to you to fill that in for yourselves.

One other point about the vignettes and illustrations used in this book. I am going to give you a lot of them. Do not do them all. Pick the ones that seem most different from your own situation first. After you've developed your skills and learned the techniques, go back and tackle the ones that feel closer to home. The closer they are to your real life, the more difficult they can be. Be good to yourselves. Start simple and keep it easy.

Read the following story about Chris and Pat.
   Look for "content" words and "process" words.
   Circle the content words and underline the process words. I've done the first several lines to get you started.

Although Pat and Chris had been together for ten years, they had never resolved their ongoing dispute about how hot or cold the house should be. In the summer Pat complained that it was too cold and in the winter Chris complained that it was too hot.

Chris: I might as well wear a bathing suit around here it is so hot!

Pat: Well, bully for you, at least I don't complain even though I have to wear five layers of clothes around the house.

Chris: Aren't you the saint! I guess it would suit you if I went around naked, huh? I am tired of this fight. Can't we figure out some compromise?

Pat: Okay. I was being sarcastic and I am really frustrated at feeling cold all the time but I just don't know what to do.

Chris: Well, how about that new kind of heater that is out? I think it heats just a small area but makes it quite warm. If we put two of them near the areas where you usually sit or work, would that help? I truly can't wear fewer clothes than I have on right now.

You will notice that you are underlining more than you are circling because most of what we say to one another involves process.

Here's another one to try:

Chris and Pat have been together for four years now. They are both in their late twenties. They rent a decent apartment in the city. They each work full time and they have one cat and one dog. Pat wants more.

Pat: I want us to have children.

Chris: We talked about this when we were going together. I thought we agreed not to have children until we were in our thirties.

Pat: I know, but I grew up in a large family and I've always imagined myself as an adult with children in my life. I am really feeling strongly about this.

Chris: Well, I am just not ready. I still agree with our original plan and I don't want to talk about it right now. I have some job possibilities that I haven't mentioned to you and they may require that we move. That is just too much stress on me to even think about our having a baby!

Pat: This issue is not going away and it is very important to me. I know it is hitting you out of the blue, but I've been thinking about it for several months now, and I felt it was time to bring it up.

Chris: Well, your timing is terrible and I am not going to talk about it anymore.

Circle CONTENT and underline PROCESS in the example above.

Consider this . . .

Anne's Reflections

Two rules:

First. No sarcasm.

This rule has worked for Bernie and me for years.

Second. Don't lecture or psychoanalyze your partner.

Lecturing and psychoanalyzing are different but they often accompany one another in that they are both styles of attempting to relate by telling your partner what you are sure he or she needs to know and will profit from hearing. As the kids say—NOT! Lecturing is easy to notice. There are clues. If you have slipped into the third person or the second person, you are lecturing. Some examples would be: "If you clean your room everyday, you will not have such a big job to do on Saturday." "I think you should consider doing . . ." "You get yourself into these messes whenever you do that. If you would just [fill in the blank] this would not happen."

Notice that a lot of these statements are sentences you might well use with children but you have not married a child. You are both adults and want to communicate with each other with respect. If you've been asked for your opinion or advice, that is a totally different matter, but if you haven't been asked, you are in danger of creating distance between yourself and your partner. Use "I" statements here. "I am very concerned about how upset you are getting. How can I help?"

"Psychoanalyzing" happens when partners offer explanations of behaviors and offer theories about how those behaviors developed. As with "lecturing," if your partner has asked you for this input, then it is not the same as psychoanalyzing. In that case it's an intimate discussion in which you have been asked to share your perspectives. That is very different from launching into a speech by saying, "I'm sure you have this problem because your father left when you were five. You have spent your whole life trying to replace him . . . etc . . . etc" Lecturing and psychoanalyzing are not helpful and usually lead to either anger or withdrawal on the part of your partner.

Week 4

CHECKING IN WITH YOURSELVES!

Are we still spending twenty minutes a day talking with each other? *YES   NO   Decided not to*

Are we still meeting once a week to have our "business meeting?" *YES   NO   Decided not to*

Have we set aside at least two hours a week just for fun and are we using them? *YES   NO   Decided not to*

5

LEARNING THE STEPS OF PROCESSING

In the first four chapters you established or changed your patterns with one another sufficiently that you have now formed habits of talking with one another every day, and you have had at least one or two weekly "business" meetings. You are also taking time to play and have fun together. Since you now understand the concepts of content and process, it is time to learn how to use your process with one another to become clearer about content issues which are problems or lead to disagreements. I call this "Processing." These are the Steps for Processing:

The Steps
1) DECIDE WHO IS GOING TO START
One of you will be the presenter and one will be the listener

2) PRESENTER
Take one topic at a time (e.g. debt)
Explain what makes it an issue for you (e.g. worry)
Say what you want

3) LISTENER
Listen to what is said
Pay attention to how you feel
Say how you feel
Say what you think is being asked for and clarify this
Respond

4) TALK UNTIL YOU REACH AGREEMENT ON A NEXT STEP

5) PRESENTER
Express appreciation

Decide who is going to start

You will be deciding who is going to begin with the first issue. This person will be the Presenter. The other person will be the Listener. Each one of you has different tasks, and the roles will change, so you need to learn each part.

Presenter
- **One topic at a time**

On the surface this looks easy. You will begin by picking one topic and sticking to it; however, if you remember your high school geometry you will recall that every theorem has its corollaries, and the corollary to "one topic at a time" is "everything is related to everything." What this means is that when one person introduces a topic, the person listening to it will almost always have other issues that are triggered by this particular topic. It is very difficult at times to stay with the topic "on the table," but do not go off topic to anything else no matter how clearly relevant it appears to be. The positive aspect of "everything is related to everything" is that it truly does not make any difference where you begin when you try to work things out. Any movement made in the direction of resolving one issue will have ripple effects on other issues. Stick to these steps and watch it happen.

• How to present an issue

Whoever presents the issue talks about the area of concern or frustration and conveys some sense of the emotion attached to it; anger, hurt, frustration are some of the more common themes here. While talking, try to use "I" language. For example:

"I get really angry every time I trip over the clothes on the floor."

Rather than:

"You make me so angry when you leave clothes on the floor."

There is a lot written in basic communication books about the use of "I" rather than "You." It is a simple technique, often amazingly difficult to stick to, but it can remove walls, such as defensiveness, almost miraculously. Review the earlier pages about "I" statements if you need to refresh your skills.

• Say what you want

The Presenter goes on to SAY WHAT HE/SHE WANTS. This is trickier than it seems. For some reason in our culture, a number of us think that if we describe a problem, the person listening should jump in and fix it without our even saying what we want done. SAY WHAT YOU WANT. BE CLEAR. BE SPECIFIC.

Listener
• How to listen and respond

This is the toughest role. Hearing words that feel like a complaint about how you are acting is difficult. It requires mature discipline to be able to hear these issues not as an assault or demand *on you* but as evidence of your *partner's* distress. **You are not responsible for that distress.** That is inside your partner, but you are being asked to change something about your style that your partner thinks might make a difference.

It is difficult to hear these words without becoming defensive, but your job is to LISTEN and to KEEP BREATHING. That's all you have to do—and it is usually plenty!

After the Presenter has finished, make sure you understand exactly what is being asked of you. "You are frustrated about my leaving clothes on the floor and you want them in the laundry basket every night before we go to bed. Is that correct?"

Once you are clear about what is being asked, it is your turn to do the talking and the other person listens WITHOUT INTERRUPTING. If you have feelings triggered inside you from hearing this issue, now is the time to say so. Saying those feelings out loud helps you clear yourself so you can respond. It is also okay at this point to mention any related issues that popped into your head while you were listening.

"It's hard for me to hear you about this issue. I'm reminded of all the times I was scolded as a kid for not cleaning up my room, and I am feeling like a kid. It's also hard for me to listen to a complaint about my untidiness when I deal everyday with the chaos in the garage created by the unsorted recyclables and the garage sale stuff."

(CAREFUL HERE. You can say what the related issue is but this is not the time to talk about it. The issue "on the table" is clothes on the floor. The temptation here is to turn this into a fight about who's sloppier rather than taking a step toward resolving an issue that can be fixed).

So you've clarified what is being asked of you. You've "cleared" yourself by saying out loud the competing internal dialogue you were having. *(Cleared means that you've carefully noted all the distracting issues and having done so, you've put them aside so you can focus completely on the issue on the table.)* Now is the time to say what you are willing to do about the request that's on the table.

"Here's my frustration. The laundry basket is on your side of the bedroom and opposite both the bathroom and the closet. I would like to try moving it to the other corner of the room, and if you are willing to make that change, I will make sure my laundry gets in there before we go to bed at night. Does that sound reasonable?"

Approaching agreement

The Listener has clarified the request, stated his/her own feelings about hearing it and has now offered an idea to change the setup in the bedroom to make it easier to comply with what is being requested.

Now it is up to the Presenter to say if this is satisfactory or not. If it is, make a simple statement such as, "Thank you for hearing me. That change is no problem for me, and I appreciate that you are willing to do this." or "Thanks. That works for me. Let's give it a try."

If the Presenter has a problem with the proposed solution, now is the time to state it:

"Thanks for trying to think this through. I'm okay with moving the laundry basket as long as it is not on the path to the closet. I don't want to trip over it. Can you see how that might be done?"

Notice that both people are now accepting that this issue needs some attention, and they are brainstorming how to make things work.

Week
5

Deciding on next steps

Who is going to do *what* next to make this change happen? Person A is going to move the laundry hamper now. In this specific example the next step is simple and easily done, but it is important to decide between you who is going to do it. Other issues can get much more complex and "next steps" may require more time.

Expressing appreciation

If the Presenter has not yet said "thank you" now is the time to do it.

Switching roles

The Presenter now becomes the Listener and vice versa. It is now the second person's opportunity to bring up a topic to discuss. It may be a related topic, like preparing for the garage sale, or a totally different topic but it is only one topic . . . follow the same steps.

The Steps

1) DECIDE WHO IS GOING TO START
One of you will be the presenter and one will be the listener

2) PRESENTER
Take one topic at a time (e.g. debt)
Explain what makes it an issue for you (e.g. worry)
Say what you want

3) LISTENER
Listen to what is said
Pay attention to how you feel
Say how you feel
Say what you think is being asked for and clarify this
Respond

4) TALK UNTIL YOU REACH AGREEMENT ON A NEXT STEP

5) PRESENTER
Express appreciation

Consider this . . .

Anne's Reflections
If either of you "wins" an argument then you both just lost. The goal in an intimate relationship is to develop solutions which both of you can live with. Neither of you wants to win. This is not about either of you alone. It is about the health and welfare of your relationship. Look for agreements which involve a little bit of give on both sides.

6

PRACTICING THE STEPS FOR PROCESSING

This section provides you with an opportunity to practice the steps for processing, using the issues of two people other than yourselves. In working with their interactions, you will learn the steps, ways to express issues and the multiple possibilities for solving situations. You will be able to do this without getting distracted by the added task of dealing with the emotions usually linked with personal issues. I want you to learn the skills well before you use them with your own issues.

The SCENARIOS: Chris and Pat are back and in four different scenarios. They need your help in getting through the steps for processing.

 #1 Early relationship issues

On the surface, Chris and Pat are dealing with issues about a pet. They are in their twenties and their relationship is pretty young. Pat's mother loved cats but not dogs. Dogs were much too much trouble. They were dirty and they shed. In Chris's house there was always at least one dog—often two or three.

Pat and Chris are getting ready to establish a household together. Chris's current dog, George, has been a good companion for five years. Pat has not lived with a pet since leaving home for college and never cared much for dogs.

If George comes into the new household, Pat wants him kept in the yard. George has always been an indoor dog, living with Chris inside the apartment. Chris does not want George out in the cold.

Use the STEPS FOR PROCESSING and follow Chris and Pat through this situation.

1) Pick ONE of Chris's issues

_____

_____

3) How would you express that issue?

_____

_____

4) What specific change would you suggest Chris request?

_____

_____

5) What might make it difficult for Pat to hear this request?

_____

_____

6) What would be one significant step Pat could offer to take?

_____

_____

For additional practice go back and answer 1-6. This time take it from Pat's point of view.

#2 Sex and intimacy

Chris and Pat are in their early forties and yet they are having sex about as often as couples in their seventies—or perhaps less often. They are both tired. They are in the stage of life during which there are lots of external demands on each of them. Neither of them is having an affair. They are both clear that they truly love each other and are committed to being together, but both sex and the related intimacy are missing from their daily lives. They are good partners and handle all that needs doing, but they are living together more like roommates. One day Pat realizes a deep sense of loneliness and decides it is time for them to talk.

Week 6

Help them have this discussion. Pat is going to go first and the issue is a sense of loneliness and separation. Take it from there and help these two out!

1) How would you suggest that Pat express the issue?

_____

_____

2) What specific change would you suggest be requested?

_____

_____

3) What is your guess about Chris's initial reaction?

_____

_____

4) What might make it difficult for Chris to hear the request?

_____

_____

5) What would be one significant step Chris could offer in the direction of what is being asked?

_____

_____

 #3 Parenting issues and religion

A "cradle Episcopalian," Chris lay in bed yet again on a Sunday morning while Pat fixed breakfast in the kitchen. It had been several years since either of them attended church, and Chris was thinking it was time. The local Episcopal church was only a mile from their house, but Pat was raised in the Quaker tradition, and a Sunday meeting was a far cry from Sunday mass. Although they had talked about this when they first got to know each other, neither realized that as they aged and had a family the differences could become an issue. Their son, Steven, was six now and hearing in school about kids who went to church on Sunday. He was starting to ask questions. Chris decided to talk this over with Pat and see what they could work out.

1) Help Chris phrase this issue here using "I" language:

_____

_____

_____

2) What specifically might Chris request?

_____

_____

_____

3) List all the issues you think Pat might have about this request (losing the quiet of Sunday mornings, raising Steven in an unfamiliar religion, etc.):

_____

_____

_____

Week
6

4) List several steps Chris and Pat might consider:

_____

_____

_____

Before we go on to help them process and come up with some decisions, let's pause and reflect on the depth of these issues. On the surface this might be about their son's religious and spiritual upbringing, but it is also about Chris and Pat. Where are each of them in their own life stages? Each of them has some significant reflecting to do, and then they can talk with each other in some depth about their religious or spiritual paths. These issues are complex, and it is a delicate task to allow the relationship to remain in balance while each partner searches and reflects. There is a potential richness when these reflections can be shared. It is a good thing they have some solid history and stability between them as a starting point so that this issue does not become divisive.

Week 6

Now let's help them process this:
Review the STEPS

1) Decide who you are going to have "go first," Chris or Pat.

2) Pick ONE issue from that person's list.

_____

_____

3) How would you express that issue?

_____

_____

4) What specific change would you suggest be requested?

_____

_____

5) From the other point of view, what might make it difficult to hear this request?

_____

_____

6) What would be one significant step in the direction of what's being asked?

_____

_____

To practice the steps go back and complete 1-6 again using different issues and trying it out from the other point of view.

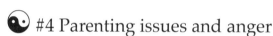 #4 Parenting issues and anger

"I said *no* and I meant it!" Pat hollered at the kids. In the next room Chris's gut tightened, thinking that this had to stop. They had agreed over and over again that disciplining the children would be handled calmly. They had talked about consistency. They had agreed and agreed and agreed . . . and here it was happening again! It was time to talk. The children were only seven and ten years old. Sometimes trying ages to be sure, but this level of frustrated, irritated and just plain loud interaction was out of line as far as Chris could see. This had to stop. It was time to talk!

Meanwhile, Pat was feeling tired after a difficult day on the job and the incessant "yammering" of the two kids was difficult to listen to. In addition, Chris was in the next room watching the evening news. What was that about? Weren't they both the parents? Didn't they both work? This had to stop. It was time to talk!

List the possible issues from Chris's point of view:

_____

_____

_____

_____

_____

_____

List the possible issues from Pat's point of view:

_____

_____

_____

_____

_____

_____

Steps for Processing—let's follow them for Chris and Pat in this situation.

1) Decide who you are going to have "go first," Chris or Pat.

2) Pick ONE issue from that person's list.

_____

_____

3) How would you express that issue?

_____

_____

4) What specific change would you suggest be requested?

_____

_____

5) From the other point of view, what might make it difficult to hear this request?

_____

_____

6) What would be one significant step in the direction of what is being asked?

_____

_____

To practice the steps go back and complete 1-6 starting with the other person's issue and answer all the questions from that point of view.

That is the end of the practice sessions. By now I hope you have a good sense of the steps to follow in processing issues with one another. Next week you are going to start with your own issues. *Use the week to think through issues you want to address.* Be gentle with one another as you shift to working on your own issues. You are both learning new ways to communicate. It takes time and it takes practice.

7

NOW-IT IS ALL ABOUT YOU!

There is nothing magical here. This is a system. It has worked for a lot of couples and it is a tool you can make your own in time. First learn the steps and follow them. Later on you may decide to change some of them to suit yourselves. This meeting time is for your own issues. Prepare in advance by deciding on a topic you would like to discuss. Each of you will come to the meeting with your own topic. Remember, you have set aside one hour and that is enough time to get started on two different issues. If you decide to focus on one person's issue for the whole hour that's fine. Just remember that the other person begins the next time.

Take a minute to review "The Steps" and then use the next couple of pages to guide you through the process the first few times.

If you get stuck, *TABLE THAT ISSUE FOR NOW.* After you read the section on dealing with impasses you can come back to that issue again and use the 1% impasse skills to help you move on. For now, put it aside.

Copy the next two pages for your use.

The Steps
1) DECIDE WHO IS GOING TO START
One of you will be the presenter and one will be the listener

2) PRESENTER
Take one topic at a time (e.g. debt)
Explain what makes it an issue for you (e.g. worry)
Say what you want

3) LISTENER
Listen to what is said
Pay attention to how you feel
Say how you feel
Say what you think is being asked for and clarify this
Respond

4) TALK UNTIL YOU REACH AGREEMENT ON A NEXT STEP

5) PRESENTER
Express Appreciation

Week 7

Processing Worksheet

Presenter: Think through how you want to present your issue. Take some time to explain what the issue is, how you feel about it and what you would like to see change. Ask clearly for what you want. Make some notes for yourself if that will help you. You can use this space if you'd like.

_____
_____
_____

Listener: Pay attention to your initial reaction as you listen. Notice anything at all that makes it difficult for you to hear. Write some of those things down.

_____

_____

_____

_____

<u>Listener:</u> *Decide how far you are able or willing to go in the direction of what is being asked. Offer to do or change as much as you think you can without resentment. Keep in mind that you can specify that this change will be on a trial basis. You can come back to it again and make adjustments if necessary.*

_____

_____

_____

_____

Week 7

<u>Presenter:</u> *Your turn to listen now. Even if your partner is not offering to do all of what you ask, try to accept any offer that moves things in your direction. Be specific about what you think is being offered and make a plan for where and when the change will start. Remember to say "thank you." Changing is difficult for everyone!*

For both of you: Congratulations!

You have completed one session of processing—but you have one more step. Before you stop, take a minute for each of you to say what you think you just decided on and make sure you are saying the same thing. Its amazing how often a couple will feel relief that something has been discussed and feel like progress has been made, but each person will have a totally different view of what has been decided. So, take a minute and be clear with one another.

Reflect on your processing session

Did you find that you needed to table an issue? Sometimes, even following these steps, you can end up stuck or at an impasse. The next tools for you to learn are skills for getting out of those stuck places. After you have practiced processing for a couple of weeks and familiarized yourselves with the "Infamous Six" topics which most couples share (and which are presented in the next chapter) we will return to the discussion of techniques, and I will teach you about impasses.

I want you to stop for now. The processing steps you just worked with take energy. Respect the effort involved for each of you and take a break. Refer to the list of "fun" things you enjoy doing together and do one of those, or just go your separate ways for a while and enjoy a few minutes alone. It may take one of you more time to recover from processing than the other. Allow for that.

Week 7

Consider this . . .

Anne's Reflections
Each time you work on an issue you should make at least an inch of progress. This has to do with processing differences. You should never have the same argument twice--ever! There are certainly some topics which will come up again and again in any relationship between two people, but if you truly take the time to talk them out, each time they come up again you should find yourselves at a slightly different starting point.

With each processing discussion, some compromise or decision should be reached which moves you at least "an inch" closer to each other. If you find that you are having the same fight over again, use it as a signal to yourselves that you need to look carefully at how you are processing. Are you shortcutting the steps? Are you making decisions but not checking to make sure you each agree about what decision was reached? Conversations with a déjà vu feeling are a signal that it is time for a little fine tuning with your processing skills!

8

THE INFAMOUS SIX

As you begin to shift to working with your own issues during your weekly meetings, I'm going to make a shift from talking about process to talking about content. There are certain content issues that most—or all—couples have to deal with. I call them the "Infamous Six," and I want to spend some time talking about them because they are often the triggers for conflict.

There have been books and books written about each of these topics. I am touching on them lightly here just to raise a few issues. If you are interested in learning more, do some reading, find a good therapist, start journaling, join a group or see what is available in your community. There are many resources to help with each of these topics. Your local library, bookstore, church or Mental Health Association should be able to help you find those resources.

Let me give you a little introduction to them here. In my clinical experience, the top six issues shared by most couples are:

◊ Sex
◊ Money
◊ In-laws

Week
8

◊ Children
◊ Household tasks
◊ Time

Notice that these topics have to do with the daily aspects of life. People who end up as a couple usually agree on major issues and share similar values, but the day-to-day rhythm of life together generates issues, which appear small on the surface but underneath have to do with control, separation, dependence and cooperation.

Neatniks marry slobs. Morning people marry night people. People who record every expense on their computer software connect with people who are apt to exclaim, "OOPS" when they discover their bank statement is not what they imagined it to be. People raised in close families who touch a lot end up with people who were raised in families where people rarely noticed who was home. That's just the way it is!

Ruling out situations of abuse and meanness, there are no moral issues here. There are no "right ways" and "wrong ways" about any of these issues; but most of us feel strongly that the way that is familiar to us is "right," and our tendency is to insist that our way be *the* way. This is when the problems start.

Two people attempting to live an intimate life together are creating a "personhood" separate from themselves. This is the personhood of the relationship. I referred earlier to this "third person" of the relationship. The relationship has its own needs totally apart from the needs of the two individuals in it. It needs balance, privacy, variety and a fair amount of stability. The task for the two people is to make decisions between themselves that are good decisions for the relationship. Compromises around so-called "right" and "wrong" ways of being in the world are possible. They can be worked out, agreed to and lived out with a generosity of spirit, or they can be argued about incessantly and become a terminal wedge between the couple or buried unhappily, creating a cold war atmosphere.

Let's look at some of the areas of life that seem to be most challenging because these are probably topics you will want to discuss with one another during your "processing" hours. It might be helpful to see that you are not the only people in the world with issues about these topics. *After reading about each topic, list issues that could be the focus of your weekly meetings.* **Often, this list is best done separately.** *There are spaces provided if you choose to do it together.*

Sex

Sex is a topic that usually gets people's attention. Most folks have opinions about sex. Many people like sex. Some people disapprove of sex. Sex is part of daily life in many ways in our culture. Sex in an ongoing intimate relationship is different from anything you read in popular magazines or books. That is because each couple establishes for themselves the balance of sex and intimacy that works for them. **"Works for them" means that they feel connected to one another, energized by one another and loyal to one another.**

Week
8

For many years I have used two expressions about sex and intimacy when talking with couples. The first is: **"Sex is the glue."** A good sexual relationship establishes a level of connection—as tight as glue—that strengthens people to withstand the demands of life, especially during the years of raising children. But my second sentence is important here, and that is: **"Sex is God's great joke."** I used to say this only to heterosexual couples because usually (not always!) the man wanted sex more frequently than the woman, while the woman wanted gentle touching and communication more than the man. Over the years in my work with same-sex couples, I have found the same pattern. One person is more interested in sex while the other is more interested in talking and being connected in that intimate way. When an impasse happens regarding a couple's sexual and intimate life, we stumble onto "God's great joke."

In order for sex to happen regularly there has to be a sense of intimacy. In order for intimacy to happen there has to be talking and gentle touching. The person who craves sex more is usually better adept at intimate talking *after* sex has happened, but the person who craves intimacy doesn't want sex until the talking has happened. That's the "joke." Somebody has to make the first move or the couple will remain stuck in this pattern and there will be neither sex nor intimate talk. And both need to happen . . . in equal measure, for the relationship to thrive.

If a couple has found the ratio of intimacy to sex that works for them, they have discovered an important secret. Each couple's ratio is different. Some nights they may want to cuddle before going to bed. Sometimes it feels important to take those last minutes before sleep to talk about the evening. Sometimes there is sex. What is important is that each person in the relationship is satisfied with the frequency with which cuddling/talking/sex happens between them. If your pattern is not nourishing both of you, it is time to talk.

Talking about sex and intimacy may be a difficult thing to do. It is so easy to get trapped into thinking, *He should know what I need. I am certainly giving her enough signals about what I want.* Time for "longhand" communication. ***Set aside one of your processing hours and tell each other what you want. Follow the steps. Speak and listen to one another and make some changes.*** Sex is good glue! It is fun. It can be good for you and it can be glue for the relationship.

Topics About Sex To Discuss At Weekly Meetings

1)_____

2)_____

3)_____

4)_____

Money

There are issues about money for the rich and the poor alike.

◊ Who earns the money.
◊ Who spends the money.
◊ Where the money is kept.
◊ How the money is spent.
◊ Where the money is spent.
◊ If the money should be spent.

The dollars may increase but the issues do not necessarily decrease. Certainly money is more of a survival issue if there is not enough of it; but what is enough is an issue in itself.

It is important to be able to talk about money and it is important to agree about how you as a couple will approach dealing with earning it and managing it. There are many books about money. There are workshops and training seminars and magazines and web sites. See if you can find one of these that you both are willing to study together. It is helpful to speak a similar language with one another when it comes to discussing money.

Use one of your processing hours to tell one another how money was handled—or not handled—in your family when you were growing up. Who earned it? Who spent it? Were you given money as a child? Was money so scarce that you experienced real hardship, deprivation or ridicule as a child?

Was money so plentiful that your parents spent it frivolously and never taught you to manage it? Was it a taboo subject in your family? Did you experience having lots of money and then having very little? Children often experience this stark contrast when divorce, death, illness or unemployment happens to the parents.

After you have shared this history with one another, take another hour and decide when and how you are going to make decisions about how finances will be handled in your shared life. Follow the processing steps. Make compromises. Make decisions. Figure out each other's strengths and use them. See if you can separate this business part of living together from the emotional part. It is a helpful distinction. Are you going to take a class together? Watch a video about it? Read the same book? Schedule time for this and do it. You may decide to suspend your weekly meetings for a while in order to work on this project with each other. Find a common language that you both agree to use when speaking about money.

Week 8

Topics About Money To Discuss At Weekly Meetings

1)_____

2)_____

3)_____

4)_____

In-laws

• **Privacy**

Do you remember that one of the words I used to describe the health of a relationship was privacy? Couples need privacy and separation from their extended families in order to develop their own rhythms of life with one another. This has to do with creating and maintaining boundaries.

It helps to have a little geography between you and your extended family. Even a block's distance is helpful. If you are living on the same land or in an apartment in the same building, find some ways to make sure you have the privacy you need as a couple and remember that your parents and/or siblings need that privacy also. Find out when they like to have their time alone and let them know when you want yours. If you are living with your parents, actively work to become participative adults in that setting. Make sure you provide a couple of meals a week. Find out what help is needed in the household and provide it regularly without being asked. Pay rent. Take care of your own children. Talk openly with your parents about the long-range picture for this arrangement. You may need to meet with them just as you do with one another, perhaps monthly, to see if there are issues that need to be worked out or patterns that need changing.

If you are the parents of the younger family that has moved in, remember that you also need a certain privacy around your relationship with one another. Both specific space and specific time needs to be reserved just for the two of you—no matter how many others move into the house. Think through how this best suits you and discuss it with your adult family members. Be clear about what you want for yourselves and your expectations of them while they are living there.

Week 8

• **Togetherness**

Family reunions are not vacations. This is true for single people as well as for couples. But the stresses of one person reentering a system they have left (on a daily basis, anyway), coupled with the stresses of another person entering a system where they have little or no history, can make for a dicey combination. Recognize that you probably have a different rhythm with your partner than you ever had with your family and that the family's tendency is to pull you back into the patterns that are comfortable and familiar to them. Keep in mind, spouses may be lonely when their mates are with family, not just because they don't share the same history, but also because the partners disappear and become different from the persons they are used to living with. **It is quite possible to get pulled into these old patterns without realizing it.**

In the best situations you might actually love and enjoy being with your family. Having listened to people talk about this for thirty years, I would say this is a gift. Many people truly love their families, but being with them takes tremendous energy. These family members—one way or another—are the people who helped you become who you are today; but the "you" you are today is not the same person they lived with. It is sometimes helpful to take a mental step backwards and watch the dynamics as they play out. When Mom says "this," Dad responds with "that." When the youngest brother enters the room, everyone gets tense. When the oldest daughter gives a suggestion, she is ignored. These are the patterns I am calling "dynamics." Every family has them. Pretend you are a visitor from another country interested in learning about their ways. See what you learn about your family's dynamics.

Week
8

You can truly become friends with your other family members, but this requires that they be able to see and respect the person whom you have become as an adult and that you do the same with them. This takes time. It takes personal awareness and an ability to view the other with clarity and compassion. It also requires having a sincere interest in how each of you is living your life now and making the effort to share some of those details and be supportive. It requires recognizing that your siblings or your parents are not automatically your friends. It requires choosing to move the relationship to a different level. Sometimes this happens. Often it does not.

It is possible to get lost in family gatherings. Roles can become confusing. Parents expect you to be their child. Brothers and sisters expect you to be their sibling. Your spouse expects you to be the partner. Your children expect you to be the parent. All of these expectations have the potential of pulling you in different directions.

The way to stay clear if you begin to get confused is to focus on the most important role in your current life. If you have children, that role is being the parent. If you do not have children, that role is being the wife, husband or loving partner. All other roles are secondary.

Your children need you to support and guide them in this wider world of extended family. Your partner needs you to remember that your current life is with him or her.

When you stay aware of this current role, you make it less likely that you will get swept up into old family patterns—old sibling competitions, worn-out or worn-down styles of relating (or not relating).

Week 8

If the visit is longer than a few hours, make sure you and your partner get some time alone. Offer to do the grocery shopping. Take a walk around the block. Take this time to remember that you two are the family unit that is most important now, even while you are with these other family members. Check in with one another and see if either of you needs anything special.

Families are not usually the enemy, but sometimes they are. If there is a history of abuse of any kind, be very careful about "visits." There is nothing casual about them. You need to be careful in protecting yourself, your spouse and especially your children even as you are as pleasant and present to others as possible. If you cannot make yourself safe in the setting, do not go and do not invite them to visit you. Hopefully, you are dealing with regular, run-of-the-mill family issues—whatever "run-of-the-mill" is!

Know that you may get ungrounded and that it takes energy to be with both your spouse and your family at the same time. Grounded means feeling confident and secure in your own skin and in your own sense of self. If you start to feel ungrounded give yourself some breaks. Stay aware. **Recognize that you and your partner will need a little time to reconnect with one another after the visit.** This is all very normal. Personally, I think it relates to the "physics" I will talk about when we focus on time and transitions later in this chapter. Everybody's got their own "forcefield" of energy around them, and when you enter that field, you bring your own energy with you. It is a bit destabilizing for everyone. Give attention to the comings and goings. They are real transitions.

Week 8

If you are the "in-law" in the situation, make sure you have been clear ahead of time with your partner about what your needs are, and find out what kind of support is needed from you. You will see things differently because this is not the family in which you were raised. Your perspectives are just as valid as anyone's; but it's quite possible that no one wants to hear them. Sorry. These folks have been dancing with each other for many years before you came on the floor. Little by little you will develop your own dance steps with them and you will build your own history. In the meantime, be friendly, be helpful and be aware of what your spouse needs from you.

If, while you are there you suddenly realize how like her mother your partner is—DO NOT TELL HER THIS! There is a delicate balance between the value of having the perspective of "outside eyes" on how the family operates and the readiness of your lover to hearing these gems of insight from a partner, however lovingly they are offered. I am going to trust that you can figure out why that is!

Your family is your family. Her family is her family. There is also a boundary around her relationship with these people who have been so integral (for good or for bad) to her growth and formation. If you must, ask her later on if she wants your input. If the answer is, "No thank you," respect that. You have only your current perspective anyway. You were not there during the history-making. For the most part, these insights are best shared when someone asks you for them or not at all.

Take a processing hour to talk with one another about each extended family and what it is like for you as the "in-law" as well as the family member. Follow the steps. One person at a time. Just listen at this point. See if there are issues that need to be addressed later and plan to do that.

Topics About Extended Family To Discuss at Weekly Meetings
1)_____
2)_____
3)_____
4)_____

Week
9

Children

Children can add delight, distress, challenge and complexity to the couple's relationship with one another. Their presence redefines "family," and the task of parenting calls for the best from each parent and sometimes can evoke the worst. Most couples manage to live through the active parenting years somewhere in the middle of that best/worst continuum and are able to create a safe environment for their children's development.

Sometimes children themselves are sources of stress to a couple, and sometimes couples stress themselves because of their differences about raising children. Some children are born with serious and challenging difficulties. If this is true of your child it is helpful to acknowledge the strain this reality can put on your relationship. If you are careful and take care of yourselves you can deepen your bond through these painful processes. The temptation is to retreat inside yourselves instead of keeping your energy, emotion and ideas out there and available to the relationship. These are complex situations and if you find yourselves with such a challenge, I would encourage you to find a counselor, a support group or some other person you trust and get support.

The more frequent situation is that couples differ on how to raise a child, and these differences are either never expressed or never resolved. It is not helpful to the child or to you to allow this tension to continue. *Using one of your process hours, discuss your priorities about your children.* For example, take time to compromise about how and when they will be disciplined. Talk through your hopes and dreams. Share with each other what you see as your child's strengths or challenges. Make agreements with one another. Follow them and review them periodically as your children age. Agree that, no matter what is going on between you, you will put aside time to talk with each other about your children.

Let me give you a couple of hints to get your discussions started in this area. The first is to remember that **parenting is not personal**. That phrase may surprise you. If you think back and remember the intensity of the moment when you saw your child for the first time you know that the connection is beyond personal. It is strong and intimate. The love you feel for your child—or even the current disgust you have toward your child because of his or her behavior—does not override the need for you to parent in a way that is not personal. Children need certain things. They need safety and security. They do well with predictability and consistency. Whoever is in the role of parent needs to provide those four things.

Your child needs to go through developmental stages, and during some of those stages you may be made to feel uncomfortable. When your two-year-old yells, "No!" after being told to do something, keep this in mind. That "no" is not personal. It may be difficult for you to hear it, but whoever is standing in the position of parenting that child at this stage would receive the same response. This is also true of your fourteen-year-old who says, "No." If you could remember that the tasks of parenting are your job description and do those tasks from a place of calm, you would find these necessary developmental stages easier to accept even though they remain difficult to endure.

When you talk with each other about rules and limits for your child, keep in mind the idea of making up **three levels of rules.** The first level contains everything you are absolutely fine with having your child do at this stage / age. This is the list of all the things he or she can do without your involvement or express permission. The last level is the list of things that you absolutely will not allow (such as getting in a car with anyone who has been drinking). The in-between level is the list of things you are going to tolerate, but you are going to roll your eyes and say things like, "I can't believe you are wearing that again." "I can't believe you want to do that, but if you insist, I will (sigh) allow it." This middle level allows the child the sense of successfully rebelling against you without you having to worry about the range of that rebellion.

Week 9

It is helpful for a child to have firm limits to rebel against, but you want these limits to be ones you feel keep him or her in the range of safety. You'll never be awarded the Oscar, but it may be the most important performance of your lives! These levels will need to change for the different stages of your child's development, and you will find that the first level's list gets longer and longer, the last level of absolutely forbidden activities will get shorter and shorter, and the middle level will change with the fads of the day.

Another influence on the discussion of child-related issues that is common in many relationships today is how the **role of stepparent** is going to be handled. If the child is very young, the stepparent might easily slide into a parenting role. If the child is older, the role of the stepparent needs to be thought through carefully, agreed upon by both adults, and introduced gradually, gently, consistently and with great respect to the child. It is possible to adopt parenting roles in your household without attempting in any way to replace the child's absent parent. The older child needs to know you respect his or her relationship with that other parent.

I close this section with these words, *"The best thing for children is to have happy parents."* This quote is from my brother. He and his wife have raised eight children, and this insight emerged for them during the process of those child-rearing years. The quote brings you back again to the focus of this book. If you feel connected with one another and use the tools you are learning here to work out your differences, you will be happier with each other. That will be good for your children.

Topics About Children To Discuss At Weekly Meetings
1)_____
2)_____
3)_____
4)_____

Household tasks

Everybody knows this is a big issue. In some relationships the division of duties and responsibilities around the house goes smoothly. One partner has certain strengths and interests and the other partner's strengths and interests are different. They complement each other perfectly—but somebody still has to take out the trash, and somebody still has to clean the toilet.

As trivial as it may seem, it is a good use of time to decide who is going to do what and how those tasks are going to be handled. This will involve compromise. It is a valid topic for your weekly business meeting. What you are looking for is a method or system that works for you. Each couple is different. The range of solutions is vast. Decide what fits you and what you can each live with.

Household Topics To Discuss At Weekly Meeting
1)_____
2)_____
3)_____
4)_____

Time

Week
9

You will notice that I put "time" as the last topic. That is not because it is the least problematic. In fact, in my experience, it is so problematic that it is the first thing I asked you to change in this book. Hopefully, by the time you read this as a topic, you have made changes in the way time is allocated so that it is no longer a major issue. If you are still talking with each other at least twenty minutes a day—setting aside an hour a week to process issues and setting aside at least two hours a week for fun—you have gone a long way toward handling "time" as an issue.

In some situations finding those regular hours is very difficult. People work shifts. Some people travel with their jobs. There are periods when couples might even live in different places for a while. In each of these situations try to find that twenty minutes a day anyway. If it can be by telephone, that at least allows you to hear one another's voices. Technology can help here—e-mail, texting and video cameras on computers that let you see each other and talk. If you do not live a rhythm of life that lets you be together once a week for a business meeting or for the two hours of fun time together, then get creative. If one of you travels, try to have some time just with each other after the return home. Children and other family or friends may need and want to be part of that return, but recognize that very soon after that initial hour you two need some time just by yourselves. Make it happen. Schedule it. Put it on the calendar.

For years I have said, "It is all about physics." When it comes to relationships, there seems to be something real about the "energy fields" around us and how they are either discordant or congruent. I am sure you've had the experience of being deeply engrossed in something that you are doing when you are suddenly interrupted— by the phone or by someone entering the room. If you have been deeply engrossed, you may sense this interruption as a very jarring experience. It is the "jarringness" that I'm talking about when I'm talking about "physics."

Week 9

Have you ever noticed that working in the garden alone is different from working in the garden with someone else? Walking alone has a different feel from walking with a companion. We often have a different energy about ourselves when we are separate than when we are together. Our days are a mix of being alone and being together. **There is a transition between "alone" and "together."** During this period our energies can get in sync with one another, but we have to allow some time for this to happen. Unlike computers and PDAs which can sync in one step, humans need a few steps and a little time.

Rituals help bridge this transition. Times of greeting and times of leaving need these rituals. A hug, a kiss, a touch, a word of greeting—any of these can be the bridge. One of the values of having established rituals of contact with one another is that the ritual helps you to make the transition from the state of separateness to the state of togetherness and connectedness.

Imagine the situation for couples who live at a distance from one another. There are lots of circumstances in today's world that might dictate this arrangement, but if the relationship is to thrive, care must be taken to attend to the multiple transitions which are part of this rhythm of life. As I write this, it is a sad reality that many couples in our country are forced into this situation because one or the other is in the military. Hopefully, by the time you read this the example will be less relevant—at least on the scale of today. Military couples often have little predictability about the transitions they have to deal with, and their control of time and schedules is more challenging than most. A less extreme example but still a challenge is when one person in the couple travels a lot and is gone for days or even weeks at a time. If you are living with either of these situations, be as creative as you can about finding times to connect with one another and allow a healthy respect for the time it might take to get into that sense of being reconnected. The transitions are very real.

Week 9

Another aspect of time that can be challenging has to do with whether you are a "morning person" or a "night person." I'm not referring to working shifts here, although if one of you is working shifts that would certainly aggravate things. I'm talking here about the contrast between people who are regular night owls—with tons of energy anytime after 10 p.m. but who are worthless at 7 a.m.—and people who prefer getting up at 5 a.m. because they can get so much accomplished at that hour even though their eyelids start to close by 8 p.m. These two types often find each other and end up as a couple. They then spend years trying to change each other before they finally accept the differences, make compromises in order to find some shared time, and, if they are lucky, find ways for the relationship to capitalize on their differences. Surely this is a situation in which the relationship can thrive, even though the compromises might not help either individual much.

Topics about Time To Discuss At Weekly Meeting:
1)_____
2)_____
3)_____
4)_____

A Seventh Issue for Many of Us

Not all of us have to face this seventh issue, so I don't include it as part of the "Infamous Six," but I do want to pause to recognize that for many couples unexpected accidents, severe hardships, chronic conditions or significant losses can present a crisis in the relationship. One idea that I have found helpful in these situations is to **accept illnesses and hardships as owned by both, not one. Each person has a different role to play, but both are equally affected.**

The impact of such events on a couple is profound. My husband recalls the time "we" had open heart surgery, and to hear him tell the story you'd think we were both wheeled down to the operating room and had our chests cracked open as a well choreographed medical duet. Even though he is the one who has two staples holding his chest together, he is accurate about it being "our " experience. I remember the day he called for an appointment with his doctor because he hadn't felt "right" when he golfed the previous week and thought he should check it out. After the appointment he walked into the office where we each practiced as therapists and said, "Our lives have just changed completely." From the beginning we both knew this was happening to "us."

Whether it is an accident, a newly diagnosed chronic condition or a disease one of you has had for years, it is helpful to see that if you are a couple, you both "have" whatever "it" is. I have worked with couples who have "had" heart conditions, bipolar disease, diabetes, cancer, hip replacement surgery, kidney stones, gall bladder attacks, hysterectomies and more. It is important to the relationship not to get into a kind of medical name calling—"his bipolar" or "her diabetes."

The medical condition impacts both of you, and if you face it together as a team, accepting the reality that your lives have changed, you are more likely to come closer together rather than to create distance. If it is "his" diabetes he can start to feel guilty that he has thrust this onto the relationship. You, his partner, can slide into thoughts and feelings of resentment at the loss of freedom and spontaneity that often accompanies a medical condition. A wedge develops between the two of you, and you begin to distance and move in different directions. You each carry the emotional reactions alone rather than bearing them together. If, instead, you share the burden, you can move on to see the areas of choice and enjoyment that are still available in life, even though "you" now have diabetes! The ability to adapt to change is enhanced when adapting is approached creatively.

All of that being said, a chronic illness impacts every facet of life. It potentially can drain all of your resources—energy, time, money, social supports. Acceptance as a team is the first step toward dealing with this reality, but the next step is learning to accommodate how you live your lives so that you can continue to live them as fully as possible. Usually there is a need for a different pace of life. This

Week 9

change of pace may be thrust upon you suddenly, or you may find yourselves sliding into it gradually.

Use the workbook. Use your time together to talk about this. Brainstorm what is possible. Tell each other what you need. You both "have" this condition but your jobs are different and communication is essential to your being able to continue as a functional team. Also, remember to take your two hours a week of fun time. Your definition of "fun" may need to expand creatively but figure out how you can each get a little break from what you are carrying.

Back to techniques

The next chapter is about impasses. It will tell you what they are, how they occur and how to get out of them. **It is the most important chapter in this book,** and now that you have had some practice working with processing your own issues, you are ready to learn about impasses.

Anyone can follow the steps for processing and work out all kinds of issues with one another as long as they do not get trapped into wanting to win, wanting to be right or wanting to control. In other words, processing is easy as long as you are not really human; but you are human. You are not a machine, a robot or a computer. You—each of you—has a history. You bring to this relationship your own particular personality, family, biases, preferences, opinions and "rules" for life. Any of these could trigger a slide into an impasse when you are dealing with a difficult topic. You may have experienced an impasse already and tabled the issue. Now you are going to learn how to get past that impasse. As long as you know these skills you can work out anything!

Week
9

Consider this . . .

Anne's Reflections

<u>Figure out your patterns.</u> Most couples have patterns of reactions when it comes to working out differences. One person really pushes to get to the bottom of things. Another wants to escape conflict. One becomes hurt and angry and wants to hide. Another becomes frightened and goes on the attack. Once you can figure out the patterns that are triggered by conflict, you can make agreements with one another about them. You can agree that if one person feels threatened, you will take a half-hour break. You can agree that even if you are frustrated not to get something resolved, you will let it go as long as your partner agrees to come back to the topic within a certain amount of time. You can agree that if one or the other feels overwhelmed emotionally, you will both take a brief time out. Figure out your patterns, and then make them work for you rather than against you.

Week 9

9

IMPASSE - AND THE 1% SOLUTION

An impasse happens when the processing is stopped. In the first example from the end of Chapter Four in which Chris and Pat couldn't agree on how to regulate the level of heat in the house, they were in danger of getting stuck at an impasse until Chris finally said, "I am tired of this. Can't we figure out some compromise?" Those two sentences unlocked the impasse. In the second example in that chapter they began to discuss whether to have children or not, and the conversation stopped at an impasse when Chris said, "Your timing is terrible and I'm not going to talk about it anymore." An impasse can be triggered by sarcasm, by unexpressed resentments or hurts, or by any number of things.

This is how an impasse is experienced. Imagine a scene out of some movie or reality show in which two people are shown running toward each other, and all of a sudden a thick glass wall drops between them. Now they are hermetically sealed on opposite sides of the wall. They can see each other, but they can't figure out how to touch. That is what being at an impasse feels like.

Usually, if we take the time to talk with one another—we connect. When we are at odds we try "working it out" with each other. We teach young children to "use their words" instead of hitting. So when talking doesn't seem to work, it is baffling and frustrating. We encourage talking and listening, but sometimes it feels as if there is a large wall between us. Everything stops. We look at each other in disbelief and cannot fathom that the other person is not understanding us. We have stumbled into our own personal Tower of Babel. We're at the United Nations without translators. All of a sudden it is as if we are speaking different languages. **The flow of communication has stopped.** This is what I mean by reaching an impasse.

When I was in training with Erv Polster, he used to say, "The cure is in the contact." **If you are at an impasse, you are trapped inside yourself and not in contact with the other person**. The cure—getting out of the impasse—happens when you are able to be in contact with some person or thing outside of yourself. For instance, if one person is 100% convinced that the way he or she sees a situation is the best and only way to see it, that individual has to reduce that percentage to at least 99%. This frees up 1% to make contact with the other. The 1% of doubt or concession on the first person's part that the second person just might possibly have a point is the 1% that is available for contact. The trick is freeing up that 1% and recognizing it when you've got it. So many times one partner will work hard to concede the 1% only to be rebuffed by the other because it is such a small step. A step is a step. Small steps are fine. They form the path out of the impasse and allow negotiation to resume. They lead to the 1% solution! The 1% can be either a place of agreement with one another about content, or a moment of emotional or physical connection with one another. In either case a connection happens and the impasse disappears.

Finding the 1% Solution

Some techniques to free up that 1% are:

◊ Speaking in longhand
◊ Brainstorming to the absurd
◊ Taking the other person's point of view
◊ Maintaining rituals
◊ Learning to translate

In this section I am going to explain each of these techniques. After reading through the explanations, you will come to three different examples of how they might be applied. Each example gives you a bird's eye view of a couple stuck at an impasse while trying to deal with some life situation. You will come with me into the therapy room and together we will help these two to find the 1% that lets them get back on track. First, read through the explanations of each technique.

◊ *Speaking in longhand* This is a phrase I have used for years to undo the "shorthand" with which so many couples learn to communicate. Anyone who has been with someone else for a few years knows that phenomenon which occurs when your partner says the exact thing you were just getting ready to say. We get so used to one another and so attuned to one another that this frequently happens. The other thing that happens is that we begin, invariably, to predict how our partner is going to act or react. We sometimes anticipate this reaction with such certainty that we proceed as if the words had already been said or the action had already been taken. This is one of the things that can lead to sarcasm. It can also lead to building up unspoken resentments. That's what I mean by the "shorthand" of relationships. Around some issues this is not a problem. It is often an asset. If you as a couple agree on certain values and techniques regarding how the children are responded to, you can confidently "assume" that your child will receive the same response from either parent. This kind of shorthand works well for the family and reflects stability. On the other hand, when you are trying to change patterns in your relationship, it is sometimes helpful to have a period of time when you **speak in longhand.**

Speaking in longhand means that you deliberately take more time with your communication, pay more attention to your partner, and use more words to convey what you are meaning or wanting. It means slowing down the process. Writing in longhand takes more effort than jotting down a note using text messaging. Speaking in longhand requires time and focus. The corollary to this would be **listening in longhand** (if you will stay with this analogy a second longer). If the communication is slowing down so it can be delivered more carefully, there also needs to be a deliberate slowing down so the listener has time to absorb what is being said before responding. Often when communication slows down in this way, things are said and heard enough differently to yield the 1% of potential agreement. That's the contact. Once the 1% is reached, the impasse is broken through and you can continue to discuss your issue.

Week
10

Remember the example in which Chris decided to discuss changing the Sunday morning patterns in the family to include going to church? Shorthand communication might have been, "We need to get our son to church on Sundays." Longhand communication would be, "I am feeling uncomfortable on Sunday mornings now that our son is beginning to ask questions about religion. I'm thinking we need to make some changes, and I'd like to set time aside for us to talk about this. Would you be willing to do that?"

◊ *Brainstorming to the absurd* Most of us learned the rules of brainstorming in school. Basically it is a technique that permits and encourages the expression of a number of solutions to a problem without discussing the quality of the ideas being expressed. If you are brainstorming what to have for breakfast, your list might include eggs, waffles, cereal, Danish, fruit and bacon. If you are brainstorming to the absurd, your list might also include fried worms, ice cream cake and chocolate-covered caterpillars. By specifying that the brainstorming is to be taken to the absurd both partners become free to suggest any kind of solution without judgment. This opens the creative process and sometimes yields a surprising 1% solution.

◊ *Taking the other person's point of view* This is the toughest of the five techniques listed above because it requires stepping out of your own point of view and seeing the issue through your partner's eyes. Here is how it is done.

If you look at each other when you are processing something and you are both able to see that you are stuck at an impasse, try switching positions. Do this literally. **Switch chairs with one another.** When you each get to your new chair take a minute to imagine that you are your partner. Reflect on what he or she has just been saying about this issue *from your partner's point of view only.* Stay with this. See how you feel. Guess how your partner feels about this issue. **Say three sentences out loud** about how you see things from this chair.

Pat might say, "Right now I'm 'Chris.' I absolutely do not want to do this. I feel cornered and resentful and it is very difficult for me to listen."

Chris might say, "Right now I'm 'Pat.' I am frustrated and tired and hurt that I have had to bring this subject up another time. I am beginning to feel defeated and hopeless."

Week
10

After you have each said your three sentences from the other point of view, ask your partner if you got any of it right. Tell one another which parts were right and clarify the parts that were not accurate.

You will notice that in order to have the above mini-dialogue you have to talk with each other. Once you are talking about this exercise with each other and have put out the energy to empathize in this way, you will have achieved your 1% of contact. **Contact does not mean agreement.** It means you are connected enough to step safely back onto that scaffolding and look again at the issue on the table.

◊ *Maintaining rituals* Rituals are moments of contact that you agree to have during each day **no matter what is happening.** They can be verbal or physical. Greetings, hugs or kisses at the beginning of the day, at the end of the day and often accompanying times of transition—leaving home, coming home. In the context of getting past an impasse, rituals sometimes melt the barriers when nothing else will. The value of having a ritual is that you agree to have that moment of contact with one another even when you are rushed, stressed or furious with one another.

Sometimes that connection is best done physically rather than verbally. Long ago, after what has proven to be the worst fight that my husband, Bernie, and I have ever had, he found a way to get us past the impasse by honoring our established ritual of kissing each other before going to sleep. We had argued all evening and gone to bed exhausted, unresolved about the issue, and angry. I remember being so angry that I turned away from him and laid on the farthest edge of my side of the bed. My face was to the wall and I was thinking about divorce! We said nothing to each other. All of a sudden I felt this small touch in the middle of my back. I stiffened and waited. Seconds after the touch he said, "I love you. I am pissed but I love you." I said the same sentences back to him, and we agreed we would "go at it"

Week
10

again the next day. We went to sleep confirming our love for one another. That gesture and those words allowed us to kiss each other and say "good night." We were past the impasse. He honored our ritual. We didn't know where we were going with the issue yet, but we had even more than the 1% necessary to know we could get there. That small touch softened the words that were said. Such touch is more likely to happen if rituals are established.

◊ *Learning to translate* Do you ever find yourself wondering if you have slipped into a zone where foreign languages are spoken because someone doesn't seem to understand what you think you are saying clearly? In that moment you are absolutely right. We do speak different languages.

Earlier in the book you both took time to examine your styles of communicating. Different styles contribute to these different languages. Some people need to hear a lot of facts and details and they speak in that way. They may even need to talk for quite a while and get the sense that the importance of those facts has been understood before they can hear what the other person is saying. Other people speak emotionally first, and if they do not feel their emotions are heard, they can't hear details and facts. Some people "see" how a situation looks and may actually visualize it in their minds as they talk. Others have trouble getting a mental picture of a situation but like to "hear" agreement before moving on with a topic.

Learning to translate is the technique requiring the most intuition to do well. Intuition means observing and paying attention to what your gut tells you about something. When you are observing someone else's language, define "language" in the broadest terms you can. Language includes all the skills, words and mannerisms a person uses to attempt to communicate. It also includes the length of time someone needs to convey their message. All of these become the package for the communication.

Some couples get stuck in an impasse with one another because they speak different languages. It is as if one is speaking Chinese and the other is speaking Italian. Each person speaks with great intensity and even clarity—but clarity in his or her own language, not the language of the partner. Sometimes this sense of a different language has to do with that different style you worked on earlier. Some people experience connection through a gentle touch on the arm. Others need to hear you say words. If you can figure out what each of your languages is, you can learn to use the other person's language to break through the impasse.

As long as you insist on staying with your own language, you cannot break the impasse. You need to build a communication bridge which uses your partner's language as well as your own—and each of you needs to learn to do this for the other. If you are the emotional speaker you need also to be able to talk about details and facts. If you are the detail/fact person, you need to learn to make statements which show that you have heard your partner's emotion. Even if neither of you does this smoothly, the other will appreciate the effort and experience the sense of being heard.

Week 10

> **Summary - Techniques for finding the 1% Solution**
>
> ◊   Speaking in longhand
> ◊   Brainstorming to the absurd
> ◊   Taking the other person's point of view
> ◊   Maintaining rituals
> ◊   Learning to translate

Let's look at three different examples of couples caught in an impasse and how the techniques could help them free themselves. Suggestion: you may want to use your next one-hour weekly business meeting to go over the first one of these and do the next two at the following meeting.

 Illustration #1 **House renovations**

Chris and Pat are in their thirties. They have taken on the task of building a house together. Because of this, they are having to make hundreds of small and large decisions everyday. Today, they are in the middle of working on the details about the kitchen.

Pat: (frustrated, and with resentment) Go ahead. Get whatever you want for a sink. I don't care. I'm tired of this discussion. Just do it your way. I know that's how it's going to end up anyway. Might as well not waste time on it.

Chris: Now you are making a mountain out of a molehill and you are pissed off. I'm going to have to pay by watching you sulk for the rest of the day.

Week
10

Notice that Pat and Chris are at an impasse here. Pat is sitting on feelings of frustration instead of expressing them—shutting down and lashing out with sarcasm at the same time. Chris retorts with a lecture and likewise slips into sarcasm. This conversation is going nowhere, and the residue of feelings could influence the rest of the day. They do not have to be stuck here. They could avoid resentment, frustration, sarcasm, feelings of martyrdom, feelings of moral superiority and righteousness. They could also make a decision and be done with it! Let's look at some ways to get them out of this stuck place, working from Pat's perspective.

Longhand

Pat: I am getting frustrated about this topic. Let me be clear about what I want. I don't care if the sink is deep or not. What I care about is that we not get stainless steel and that we get a faucet that is flexible and high enough that I can get the large pot under it when I'm washing it.

Chris: Well, what I want is a double sink. I want to be able to have the two sinks to work in and I want plenty of counter space on either side. I do not care about the faucet height, but I want a spray that is easy and reliable to use.

Pat: Okay then. We want a double sink with a high and flexible faucet and a good spray, and we are looking at anything other than stainless steel. Do we agree?

Chris: Yep. One less decision to make!

Make up your own version using the longhand technique in this example, by working from Chris's perspective. Take this phrase and express it in clear longhand:

"I'm going to have to pay by watching you sulk for the rest of the day."

Longhand:

_____

_____

_____

Remember: longhand communication is plain, simple, even dull or boring. It is not clever; but it is clear, and it uses more words than shorthand.

Week
10

Brainstorming to the absurd

Chris: Looks like we are stuck here, and I don't want us to ruin the day. How about if we brainstorm this issue?

Pat: Okay.

Brainstorming the issue of the kitchen sink area:

- put an extra sink in the island
- put in a mobilized sink
- buy an antique laundry tub and put it in the center of the kitchen!
- get gold-plated hardware
- get two sinks but one of them very deep
- put the laundry area adjacent to the kitchen so if we needed a deep sink, we could use the one we put in there
- get a granite top with two built-in sinks
- get a water purifier and external spouts on the refrigerator
- get a long hose attachment to hook up to the outdoor spigot!

Week 10

Chris or Pat: Let's go through this list and see if we can agree on any of the options.

Chris or Pat: I don't know about granite but I like the idea of having the sinks built into the counter top so they are not stainless steel. I don't want the external water on the refrigerator, but I think we need to look at flexible faucets that will satisfy what we each need and want.

Chris or Pat: I certainly don't want a laundry tub in the kitchen but it is an interesting image to picture one in the garden as the basis of a fountain!

Remember: there is no judgment in brainstorming. Any idea gets to be included in the list!

Pick something around your own house (something small!) that the two of you would like to see changed and brainstorm the options. Remember to brainstorm to the absurd!

*Topic:*_____

_____

Brainstorming Ideas:

1)_____
2)_____
3)_____
4)_____

(Make the list longer if you can. Sometimes the tenth or fifteenth idea is the best!)

Taking each other's point of view

Let's review the initial point of impasse:

Week 10

Pat: (frustrated, and with resentment) Go ahead. Get whatever you want for a sink. I don't care. I'm tired of this discussion. Just do it your way. I know that's how it's going to end up anyway. Might as well not waste time on it.

Chris: Now you are making a mountain out of a molehill and you are pissed off and I'm going to have to pay by watching you sulk for the rest of the day.

If Chris and Pat are going to try the technique of taking each other's point of view to get out of this stuck place, they will first exchange seats, and then each will take a turn saying three sentences from the other's point of view.

Chris (as Pat):

"I am getting worn out with this project."

"I am resentful that Chris is holding us up."

"I am frustrated that we cannot move on here."

Pat (as Chris):

"I am frustrated that I have to wait for Pat's moods to pass to get anything done."

"I am getting worn out with this project."

"I think these are all small decisions which we should be able to make."

Looking for the 1% point of agreement here, Pat and Chris might focus on the fact that they are both getting worn out and declare a break—long enough to share a cup of coffee or watch the morning TV show. Or they might notice that both of them are feeling frustrated and agree to table those feelings and move to brainstorming or saying in longhand what they each specifically want to have in this part of the kitchen.

It does not make any difference which direction they choose here. Once they are talking directly with each other they have found the 1% point of agreement. They are unstuck. They are out of the impasse and can move on in their discussion.

Taking one another's point of view is the most difficult of all of these techniques.

Why do you think that might be so?

_____

_____

_____

Consider the effort involved for Chris and Pat in this example. What is the barrier Chris has to overcome to "be" Pat?

_____

_____

_____

What is the barrier Pat has to overcome to "be" Chris?

_____

_____

_____

It takes self-awareness and discipline to do this technique but the effort of putting yourself in someone else's shoes usually yields a sense of compassion and a softening of the heart toward the other. It is worth the effort if you are so stuck that the easier techniques do not work for you.

Try it yourselves! Pick a topic you disagreed on in the past but which is fairly small and has been resolved. (Beware the bar of soap phenomenon! Sometimes small things aren't really small.) Let's say one of you wanted to grab fast food for dinner the other night and the other wanted to stop by the deli section at the grocery store instead. See what I mean? Look for small! (You can use this illustration and pick a side if you want!)

Week 10

Say one sentence about what you would really have preferred. For instance, "I really wanted to try the new nonfat yogurt at the fast food place because I have been dieting all week and I wanted to splurge." Or, "I have been watching the budget this week and I know the grocery is having a special on the rotisserie chicken."

Now switch chairs. *Take a minute sitting in that new chair to "feel" yourself into being the other person. Sit the way he or she sits for instance. From the point of view of this seat say three sentences about how you feel and what you would like to see happen.*

Go back to your original chairs and let each other know how they did at understanding your position. What did they get right? What were they missing?

That's it! You've done it! (Do you get a clue how challenging this could be in a situation that was not yet resolved and about which you both had strong feelings and opinions? It is definitely work, but it is often effective when other efforts are not.)

Next let's look at how the techniques of rituals and translating might help out in Chris and Pat's kitchen scenario.

Rituals

If Chris and Pat have already put in place rituals of contact these can help to stimulate moments of 1% to work with. "Okay. We are obviously not going to figure this out right now, but I believe we can. I'm going to run some errands, and hopefully, we can talk again when I come back. Is that okay with you?" These words followed by a kiss and a hug (their established ritual for moments of transition— "goodbyes" and "hellos") could soften both of their attitudes and prepare them for a longhand conversation later.

Review your own rituals with one another. List the ones you do regularly:

_____

_____

_____

Are there some rituals you used to do and might like to reestablish? List them here: _____

_____

_____

As you read this section do you find yourselves acknowledging that you haven't really established rituals of contact with one another? If so, reread the explanation of rituals earlier in this chapter and decide on three rituals that you would like to add to your daily lives:

1)_____

2)_____

3)_____

Translating

If you look at the initial dialogue you can guess at the differences in Chris and Pat's styles. Pat is much more into specifics about this kitchen, and Chris seems to be reacting more to the feelings of their exchange. If we think of this as "different languages" then we'd guess that Pat needs to hear specifics about sinks and countertops and Chris needs to hear more about feelings. As long as Pat is talking about sinks, Chris is not hearing anything. As long as Chris is talking about feelings, Pat is not hearing anything. If they know this about their styles, one or the other of them can "translate" the conversation. Pat can learn to speak about feelings and Chris can learn to talk about sinks!

Week 10

Chris: I have been really frustrated and hurt, but I realize you need for me to focus on the specific kinds of sinks and countertops that we need to look at, and so I will put aside my feelings for now and we can talk about those things. Later on I want to talk about how we got stuck here and I hope you will do that; but for now, show me the info about the sinks and let's make some decisions.

Pat: Yes. Let's do that. I will get the brochures. We've already narrowed it down to three or four choices so I think we can make a decision here. I agree that we need to talk about how we get stuck and don't seem to understand each other, but I appreciate your tabling that until later on.

Remind yourselves of your own styles of communicating. As you consider this idea of translating in more depth, is there more you want to say to each other about your styles? The clearer you are about your own style, as well as your partner's style, the easier it is going to be to use this translating technique to get out of an impasse.

Before going on to the next chapter, stop and consider how you did with each of the techniques in this first illustration.

1) Which technique did you find the easiest?

_____

2) Which technique did you absolutely not like?

_____

3) Which technique seems to best fit the two of you as a couple?

_____

4) Which technique did you find useful but difficult? (As in, more practice might help and might be worth it.)

_____

If you have managed to do all of the above in one sitting it may well be time for a break. Stay with the one-hour limit if you are doing these during your meeting time. Save the next two examples for another time. If you have time to spend at this point, consider what you've just done. Learn a little more about the techniques by reviewing your work, and appreciate the effort involved in trying to learn this new way of relating!

CHECKING IN WITH YOURSELVES!

Are we still spending twenty minutes a day talking with each other? YES NO

Are we still meeting once a week to have our "business meeting? YES NO

Have we set aside at least two hours a week just for fun and are we using them?
YES NO

If you are using the motivational envelope, this would be a good time to check on the amount of savings you have in the envelope and to begin to brainstorm (perhaps, even to the absurd!) about how you will splurge with that money.

Week
10

Amount saved so far $_____.

If you are using a different reward for yourselves as a motivator, make some comments here about how that is working.

_____

_____

_____

_____

10

PRACTICE WORKING WITH IMPASSES

In this chapter you will get more practice learning the techniques you will need to use to get yourselves out of an impasse situation. We will use two more Chris and Pat illustrations. Before getting into their issues again, however, try the following exercise and have some fun with these techniques. Be as outlandish as you can. The purpose here is to concentrate on the techniques themselves. It may seem silly. It is meant to be silly. You can learn just as easily while you are laughing as you can while you are crying, and it is more fun, too.

Week 11 Have you ever heard of football players taking lessons in dance? By stepping off the field they learn how to move with greater ease on the field. In this exercise you are stepping off the field of serious problem solving and letting yourselves concentrate on the movements or techniques in a lighthearted way.

Take some time with this first exercise so that when you return to Chris and Pat's worlds the skills involved in getting out of an impasse situation will come to you with ease. Ultimately you will want to have that ease to use with each other when you confront an impasse in working on your own issues. The pages between here and there are for you to hone your skills. First, have some fun!

Playing with impasse techniques

Let's have some fun with impasses. Pick one of the following fictional or historical couples, put them in an impasse and then use the techniques to get them out. I'll walk you through this.

First: Pick your couple from this list or come up with one of your own (notice that it does not have to be a real couple—pair any two historical or fictional characters).

∆ Hansel and Gretel
∆ Leia and Luke
∆ Raymond and Rosa Parks
∆ George and Martha Washington
∆ Emily Dickinson and Sue Gilbert
∆ Abraham and Sarah
∆ Hermione and Harry

Your Couple_____

Second: Put your couple into a difficult dilemma that is likely to cause them to get stuck. For instance, Hansel and Gretel may differ about leaving bread crumbs or pebbles along their way; or Abraham and Sarah may be deciding about birth control. Be absurd here. Have some fun. Give them some ridiculous problems. Get them stuck and get them out. Describe their situation:

Week 11

_____

_____

_____

Third: *Walk them through the techniques and get them out of this!*

>   1-Speaking in longhand
>   2-Brainstorming to the absurd
>   3-Taking each other's point of view
>   4-Give them some saving rituals
>   5-Translating

How the three couples approached this:

Sam and Sandy picked Hansel and Gretel and put them into an argument about whether to be nice to the witch or trip her. They started with "brainstorming" since it seemed like the technique which would be the most fun.

Judy and David had Martha Washington complaining to George about where he put his wooden teeth at night. They worked with Martha and George to get them to establish new evening "rituals" together.

Jean and Jackie decided to see if Abraham and Sarah could come up with agreements about parenting using the "longhand" technique.

Consider this . . .

Anne's Reflections
While working on getting through impasses you will become more aware of your particular "triggers" which lead you into impasses in the first place. At that point you can begin to actively prevent them from happening. One way to do this is to attribute benign intent.

<u>Attribute benign intent</u> means giving the other person the benefit of the doubt that whatever they have done or not done/said or

not said was an action or word which came from at least a neutral place inside them. They are not setting out to make life more difficult for you. Their "intent" is to make things go well, help out, or, at the very least, as the Hippocratic oath says, do no harm. We are sometimes able to attribute benign intent toward strangers much more readily than we are toward our intimate partners. We too often jump to the conclusion that our partner's intent is anything but benign.

Here's the day I had yesterday: I came home from walking the dog to find that my husband had locked me out of the house. Later we went out for a quick lunch together on our way to take the car in to be serviced. I was handed the wrong entree at the lunch counter, and we had to wait for mine to be recooked, making the schedule tight for getting the car in at the appointed time! Later, after running errands together, we drove back in the second car to pick up the one being serviced. Things were hectic at the auto place, and it took quite awhile for me to find out what was happening with our car.

From time to time I'd signal to Bernie across the parking lot by shrugging my shoulders and lifting up my hands as if to say, "I have no idea what's happening here." I finally found someone who told me the car would take an additional forty-five minutes to fix, so I was leaning toward waiting until the next day to pick it up. When I went out to the parking lot to discuss this with Bernie, I found that he had left. He evidently interpreted my last "shrug" to mean things were okay. Here I was stranded at the auto place in a crowded room where at least five people were talking on their cell phones while I sat and waited for the car. I eventually got home, and as we were fixing dinner and unpacking the dishwasher, somehow or other a glass fell and splintered into slivers all over the kitchen and dining room, and we had to get out the vacuum cleaner to suck up the slivers before the dog started to investigate.

Week 11

Reading over that summary, can you locate all the places where there was potential for blaming? Potential for anger, hurt, disappointment, frustration? The value of ATTRIBUTING BENIGN INTENT is that there is a mitigating thought between the event and your response to it which allows some choice about how you respond. If you pause and attribute benign intent you will be less likely to spark a fight which can escalate into something else. Whose "fault" was any of what happened in my life yesterday? Were not all of those things little in the scheme of life . . . and yet, if the relationship between us had not been at a good place, any of those incidents could have caused painful reactions. Attributing benign intent acts as a brake on your responses. It allows you time to breathe—to exhale—to let it go. It is a very helpful personal exercise to practice during tense times. Life periodically brings tense times; that's just how it goes.

Now you are ready to return to the worlds of Chris and Pat. In these next two examples you will see how it is possible to confront an impasse around big life issues as well as issues triggered by the everyday. The first illustration finds Pat and Chris dealing with sensitive life transition issues.

 Illustration #1 **Dealing with aging parents**

Week 12

Chris's mother is 86 and has been living with her older sister who died recently at the age of 89. They had managed well together for almost twenty years, but when her sister died Chris's mother lost the person who took care of cooking. She had long since lost interest in doing this herself and no longer remembered how to do it. Chris and Pat are both concerned about this situation but differ sharply about what needs to happen. They both agree something needs to be done but find themselves at a difficult and painful impasse about this issue. Let's listen in and then see if we can help them with this.

Pat: I know your mother is alone now, but once again you are exaggerating what needs to be done and making it a huge crisis when it doesn't have to be. As usual, you are putting something else in the way of our being able to have time together. First it was the children, then your career and now you are proposing that your mother live with us. You have two brothers who actually live closer to your mother than we do, but you are playing the family martyr here, and once again I am left in the dust! And when she gets here, who is going to end up doing all the work? It is not going to be you; it is going to be me. I cannot believe you already offered an invitation to her without talking to me about it. You have no regard for my feelings. You are taking me for granted. Well, this time I'm not going along. You are going to have to choose between your mother and me.

Chris: She is my mother and it is my duty to provide for her. You are being selfish; and as usual you are obviously jealous of my time and attention. This is just how you were when the children lived with us, and it is the same attitude you had when my boss wanted me to travel for the job. You always want to be #1. Where is there room for what I want? If you cannot be mature enough to see what we need to do here than I guess I WILL have to choose my mother instead of you. It is obvious you are too self-centered to help out.

Okay. This is an impasse about a big issue and it is bringing up all kinds of related issues for each of them. Looking at their conversation there are clues for us about how they got stuck at this place. For Pat there are some stage-of-life-issues, such as what life could be like now that the kids are gone. There are also feelings about not having been consulted, and there is frustration because Chris assumes only they can help out when obviously there are two brothers who could.

In addition, Pat is not feeling appreciated, is hurt and angry and has issued an ultimatum because of this frustration.

From Chris's point of view this is about duty (perceived rules about how one should live), and there is also evidence of past unresolved issues about Pat ALWAYS wanting to be #1. There also could be some misdirected anger at not being able to live life the way an empty nester might want.

Let's use the techniques and see if we can get anything clarified here. Remember we are looking for the 1% to work with. They do agree something needs to be done, but they do not have 1% agreement on what could and should happen. That's the 1% Pat and Chris are going to find, using the five techniques. Let's see how they do.

Longhand

Pat: First of all, I am angry that you did not consult with me before making this offer to your mother and to your family. I feel disregarded and I don't like you to 'disrespect' me.

Chris: I am sorry about that. I was so caught up in my concerns for my mother and my frustration at how slowly my brothers seemed to be moving in comprehending how serious this could be that I just jumped in. I did not mean to ignore you or not respect your feelings. I figured we could talk about it later. I realize I could have waited to talk with them until I talked with you.

Week 12

Pat: Apology accepted. Now can we brainstorm this issue?

Chris: I'm not quite ready for that. I know you were hurt and angry but I also am angry that you issued an ultimatum. It is not like you to talk that way and I was stunned to be put in a bind that way.

Pat: I was just frustrated and pissed. I never should have put it that way and I hope you know I did not really mean it.

Chris: Can we agree—no more ultimatums no matter what?

Pat: Yes. Can we also agree no more one-sided decisions about what 'we' will take on or offer to anyone about anything, other than the occasional batch of cookies for a bake sale or something of equally small importance?

Chris: Agreed. Absolutely. Now let's brainstorm.

Brainstorming to the absurd:

- Mom could stay where she is and we could hire a cook.
- We could look into a program that delivers meals to the house.
- Each of the brothers could take turns providing at least two meals a week.
- We could fly up there once a month, do a whirlwind weekend of cooking and leave meals in the freezer.
- We could hire a personal chef for her!
- We could move Mom here and see if she will work with us financially to build a room on for her.
- We could buy a truck of military rations (MREs) and send them to her!
- We could build a cottage in the back yard.
- We could convert the living room into a studio apartment layout for her.
- We could ask both brothers to meet with us for a family brainstorming.
- We could ask Mom what she wants (. . . there's a good one!).
- We could ask Mom how she would make this work on her own— what help she could get from family and friends in the area—what skills she still has in the kitchen . . .

Week 12

Chris: Well, I think we came to the starting point at the end of this list. How could I have charged ahead without even asking Mom what she wants or how she sees things might work?

Pat: I agree, and I also think spending a little time with your brothers and your mom might give us all a chance to brainstorm this together.

Taking each other's point of view:

Reread the initial dialogue to refresh your mind about the impasse, and then let Pat and Chris start at that point using this technique. Remember they are looking for three sentences each from the other person's point of view. Pat and Chris switch chairs and Pat begins:

Pat (as Chris):
  "I am worried about my mother."
  "I am frustrated with Pat for putting up roadblocks and especially for making an ultimatum."
  "Deep down inside I also yearn for us to have some free time together now that the kids are gone."

Chris (as Pat):
  "I am really disappointed that we will not be able to have the free time together that we have looked forward to for the past few years now that we are going to be taking care of Chris's mother."
  "I get frustrated and feel powerless when Chris acts like a martyr and like everyone's slave."
  "I am angry."

Week
12

See if you can see the 1% point of contact in the dialogue above. How would you phrase that? _____

_____

It seems to me that the point of contact is that they can realize that each of them is disappointed at the prospect of tabling the plans they'd had with one another for some free time. Maybe they need to brainstorm how they are going to take care of themselves as a couple and hold onto some of this joint dream before plunging into problem-solving Chris's mother's situation. At any rate, they have reached a 1% point of contact and that means there can be connection between them; and THAT means they have freed themselves from the impasse!

Rituals

Ever since the kids left home and Chris and Pat have each been working fewer hours, they have instituted a morning ritual during which they eat breakfast together and then sit on the couch beside each other watching one of the morning TV programs. They do this every day, and they hold hands while watching. Then they kiss each other and go about their day's routine. It is a ritual that would be difficult to initiate now, since they are at this impasse, but because the pattern is set and they have agreed to spend that time with each other—no matter what—it provides them a point of connection . . . and that's the 1%!

Translating

Glancing back at the dialogue, look this time for differences in style and see what you notice.

Week 12

As I look at the argument, this is what I notice. Pat speaks from emotion first, and Chris speaks from the point of view of logic and duty. Chris seems to feel secure lecturing about how Pat has not measured up. Pat moves from one topic to another but consistently chooses words that reflect feelings. Both of them tend to enjoy a bit of hyperbole: "Once again you are exaggerating." "You have no regard for my feelings." "You are obviously jealous." "You always want to be #1." To translate, Pat needs to speak more from the head, and Chris needs to confirm that Pat's feelings have been heard.

Chris: I know you are deeply disappointed that we will not be able to move ahead with our plans, and I completely agree that I should not have talked with my family before discussing this with you. I do love you, and I appreciate all you do for me and for us. I did not mean to ignore you. I got caught up in my mother's issues, and I got lost in all of the possible obstacles and her needs. I am sorry to have left you out. I need your help.

Pat: Thank you. I appreciate that you understand my feelings, and I do realize that this crisis with your mom has been overwhelming to you. I think I can help. I've been giving this some thought, and I have some ideas I'd like to tell you about if you think you can listen. They are a little different from the route you've been considering. I will cooperate with that route if we both decide it's best, but I'd like you to hear the plans I've been turning around in my mind. I even think I've got a way we can have part of what we had planned on for ourselves as well as take care of your mother's needs.

Chris: I am ready to listen to that! If we can figure out what to do for Mom I promise to spend time brainstorming with you about our own plans and hopes for these years, okay?

 Illustration #2 **Household chores**

We have looked at the complexities of house building with Chris and Pat. We have considered the deeply difficult choices related to having aging parents. Now let's see how impasses can happen even with the mundane everydayness of life.

Chris: Between all your golf games and fishing trips, you are never here on the weekends and I am left with all the chores to do. We talk about this over and over again, and you never follow through with anything we agree to do. You are selfish and lazy and you expect to be waited on. I am not your personal slave and I am tired of you acting as if I am!

Pat: I golfed once last weekend and I haven't been fishing for three months. I don't know what the deal is with you. I have suggested that we do housework in the evenings after work but you just complain that you are a morning person and are exhausted after work. Also, when I vacuumed last week, you gave me a thousand 'suggestions' about how I needed to do the job. I'm not stupid, and I wasn't born yesterday. I lived quite well on my own for many years before I even met you, and the Board of Health never condemned my apartment. Get off your high horse and stop lecturing me. I am tired of hearing it!

The impasse in this illustration occurs because that invisible wall has gone up between Chris and Pat. Each one is seeing the situation from an entirely different perspective, and each has a set of legitimate issues needing to be addressed. We are meeting them at this point in their attempts to process, but my guess is that they did not follow the steps of processing. It has not been decided between them who goes first and whose issue is going to be addressed first. That might be a clue for helping them to untangle this mess they've gotten themselves into. Remember, their job is not to solve the problems. It is simply to dislodge themselves from this impasse. Once free of the impasse, they will be able to move through their issues and resolve them.

Week
12

Longhand

Chris: I am feeling burned out and frustrated about getting the chores done around the house. I need some help on the weekends and I feel that you are never here to help me when I need you.

Pat: It is true that I hate to do housework on the weekends. If I'm not golfing or fishing, I am very good at coming up with distractions for myself. I am willing to work on these tasks during the week, but I get really angry when you correct me and try to tell me how to do things. I feel five years old when you talk to me that way.

Chris: I think we are going to get lost in this conversation again if we don't pick one of these issues and stick to it. I agree that they are related, but I'd like for us to talk about one issue at a time. I am willing to start with yours if you want.

Pat: Well, you brought the subject up in the first place so why don't you go first? Let's review the processing steps and go through them with you beginning with the first issue. I do want to talk about my issues, too, but I can put them aside for now.

Chris: Okay. Thanks. Here is my issue: I want some help in getting the housework done.

Week
12

Notice that by getting specific about the "content" of each of their issues they were gradually able to realize that they needed to be clearer about their "process" and made a decision to go back to Step One in the processing steps. This clarity gets them out of the impasse and on the way again!

Brainstorming to the absurd

We can pick either person's issue to brainstorm, but let's start with Chris's since Chris is the one who initiated this dialogue.

The issue is how to get some help with the housework:

- We could spend ten minutes every morning and evening on the day's mess.
- We could hire someone to come in twice a week.
- We could make Saturday morning cleanup time and then go out to lunch afterwards.
- Pat could work on housework two evenings a week and Chris do the weekend part.
- We could buy one of those new robots on the market which will do the vacuuming for us.
- We could see if computer technology exists yet to automatically start different cleaning tasks for us.
- We could clean the house without wearing any clothes and see where that takes us!
- We could turn on the CD in one room, the radio in another and play a DVD in the third and see how much of each we could remember after two hours of cleaning.
- We could get rid of half of our furniture and all of our rugs so there is less to clean.
- We could move into a tent and never have to vacuum again!

Week
12

Pat: Looking over this list I see we have certainly gone to the absurd, but I see a few ideas that might actually work, do you?

Chris: I certainly do. Let's see which ones we agree are reasonable and begin talking about those.

Taking each other's point of view

Reread the initial dialogue to refresh yourself on the issues. In this section, Pat and Chris switch chairs and Pat begins:

Pat (as Chris):

"I don't like that Pat goes away so much on the weekends."

"I feel ignored."

"Taking care of household things frustrates and tires me."

Chris (as Pat):

"I don't like doing housework."

"I hate when Chris tells me how to do things."

"I am tired of hearing these complaints."

Remember in this technique, part of what happens is that each person gets to "try on" the feelings and issues from the other's perspective. This sometimes leads to a softening of one's own perspective and helps each person get to a point where listening is actually a real option. It is also about trying to find a point from which they might begin to talk again instead of staying stuck. In this illustration that "content" point might be that they are both tired of housework.

Rituals

One ritual that Chris and Pat have put into place is sitting together at the end of the work day and talking with each other before fixing dinner. They have already hugged "hello" and now, if the weather is pleasant, they often sit on the front porch. If weather is not pleasant, they just sit at the kitchen table and talk. With both of these rituals in place, it is going to be difficult to stay stuck in an impasse. In this case they will need to make a "deal" with one another so that they do not use the evening time to discuss this issue. This is their time to talk about the day and that's all. In honoring that ritual they will connect again and find a base from which to return to the troubling issue of housework.

Translating

Looking at the initial dialogue again, I think Pat is the more action-oriented person who can work a full day and still have energy for doing more in the evenings. And Pat seems to have more interests which can be pursued alone or with other friends. Chris does not appear to be an evening person at all. Also, much of Chris's focus seems to be on time spent with each other and possibly wishing to be more included in Pat's life. "Translating" in this case may be more about styles of living than ways of talking. They both seem able to talk about feelings as well as specifics, and they are each quick to make accusations against the other.

Pat: Chris, I would like to spend more time having fun with you on the weekends. I am willing to take over some of the household tasks, and we can talk about which ones they might be, but I want to do them in my own way, and I do not necessarily want to do them on the weekends. In fact, I'd rather stay up late on Friday night cleaning than have to face that on Saturday morning.

Chris: You are right that I should not treat you as if you were a child. I know you can clean adequately. We just have different standards. If you will take over the tasks I care less about, I will not pay attention to how you do them, but please don't do them Friday evening. I am just too tired then to have that much activity going on. I can work around any other evening. I too would like for us to plan something fun just for ourselves on the weekend.

Week 12

Consider this . . .

Anne's Reflections

<u>Coming home does not mean you can forget all the skills you have used out in the world all day long.</u> It is an amazing phenomenon, isn't it? We often do not bother using our well-developed social skills with the people we say are the most important people in our lives. Home is too often seen as the haven in which we do not have to be polite, considerate or helpful. We do these things "out in the world" because we have learned that the world requires such behavior if we want to keep our jobs, gain the cooperation of a neighbor on a project or protest a new tax at city hall; but when we come home we have the attitude that we don't have to "do" that "here" because this is home. Somehow we shouldn't have to be polite to our lover. There is certainly some truth embedded in this thinking. Hopefully being at home contributes to a sense of ease and contentment. If you had to be too careful about everything you said in an intimate relationship it would make you rethink the relationship.

On the other hand, crassness, harshness, abruptness and other more extreme behaviors like shouting, cursing and releasing verbal harangues just do not belong in the home any more than they belong out in the world. <u>Speak to each other with at least the same respect one would speak to a stranger</u> is a corollary of the above, isn't it? Enough said.

Copy the next pages and use them when you need them.

Impasse Resolution Worksheet

You are at an impasse yourselves now. Stay calm. Be patient. Take one step at a time and work your way out of this impasse. Try all of the techniques or pick the ones you know work best for you.
If you can, state each point of view clearly:

_____
_____
_____
_____

Speaking in longhand

Take your time. Speak clearly and slowly. Spell out your feelings and issues to each other. Try to listen with "soft ears." Remember, longhand is not clever or witty or showy. It is simple, often dull sounding. Just be as plain as you can be. If you find a 1% point of agreement or connection write it here:

_____
_____
_____
_____

Brainstorming to the absurd

Week
12

Take a piece of paper . . . or two pieces of paper . . . and write down as many solutions or options as you can think of. Be absurd. Go to the extremes. Be funny. Be silly.

Now, go back and look at your lists. Are any of the ideas helpful? Do you agree on any of them?

Taking the other person's point of view

1. Switch chairs.
2. Take a minute to "be" your partner and see things from that perspective.
3. Say three sentences about how you feel and what you think from this perspective.
4. Tell each other how well your point of view was presented. Talk about what it felt like to be in one another's shoes. If you find a point of contact go back to one of the previous two techniques and see if either one will work now.

Rituals

List some of your daily rituals as a reminder to yourselves.

_____
_____
_____
_____

Translating

Say out loud what you know your own styles and "languages" to be. Listen to each other.

Week
12

Each of you complete one of the sections below:

State your issue in your partner's "language":

_____
_____
_____
_____

State your issue in your partner's "language":

_____

_____

_____

_____

What do you notice that you agree on?

_____

_____

_____

_____

Go back to either *Longhand* or *Brainstorming* and see what ideas you can come up with from there.

If you are still stuck, still at an impasse, call a temporary truce. Table the issue and agree when you will come back and try to talk about it again.

If that doesn't work you may want to consider seeing a relationship counselor. Sometimes outside ears can hear things differently!

11

IMPASSE TRIGGERS

It is our very uniqueness which often gives rise to an impasse. We come into a relationship with a preset sense of self and personality. The life experiences that contributed to forming that self are often the source of triggers within us that can lead to our reaching an impasse with our partner. Prior relationships impact us and often live on in us, almost as if we are accompanied through life by personal "ghosts." The family that shaped us in our earliest years taught us rules that we may have incorporated rigidly but that we discover in adulthood need to be more flexible. In this chapter we will first examine the power of ghosts in our relationships. After that we will discuss the persistent influence in our lives of early family experiences.

Family influences and ghosts are very powerful in us, often because we are unaware of their presence. The more we can learn who the ghosts living within us are and become clearer about the messages we learned in our families, the more we equip ourselves to handle processing issues with one another, and the less likely we are to get stuck at impasses.

Part One - Ghosts

When I was working in my psychotherapy practice, I would routinely inquire about ghosts who might live in the household. I wasn't referring to ghosts that go "boo" in the night. I was referring to the phenomenon that occurs when someone you are with acts or speaks in a way so similar to someone else who has been in your life that you react as if you were with that other person again.

Many times the ghost is a former spouse. Often, it is a parent or a sibling. A younger sister who was teased cruelly by an older brother while growing up might find herself reacting with excessive hurt and anger when her husband says something she perceives as demeaning. "Are you wearing that again?" could be a neutral comment or a thoughtless criticism, but it is not usually a comment warranting an angry and tearful response.

Some ghosts are very benign. My husband's mother has "been with us" periodically during our marriage. Initially she was pretty powerful, but at this point the only real problem we have with her is that she "makes" us buy twice as much food as we really need if we are having a party! Other ghosts are not as benign.

I'm going to teach you some techniques to identify and get rid of your ghosts, but pay attention to how you feel when you identify them. If you start to feel anxious, tense, frightened or sad, respect that signal from within yourself and STOP! You are getting a message that this particular work needs to be done with someone else present. Find a qualified therapist to work with you.

Week
13

If you do not have such strong messages from your inner self, then move ahead with the steps listed below. A clue to finding a ghost in your relationship is to look at any responses you have that are a bit more emotional than they might need to be. If you notice such a response in yourself or—more likely—if your partner notices it, this is how to begin working with that response:

Ask yourself some questions:

◊ *Who does this situation remind me of?*
◊ *How old was I when I was with that person?*
◊ *Were there circumstances in that situation that left me less powerful to act in my own defense?*
◊ *Was I too young?*
◊ *Though older, did I legitimately fear for my safety?*

These questions will lead you to identifying the ghost. Use this space to answer those that are relevant:

_____

_____

_____

Name that ghost! There is an old Irish saying that a ghost will follow you until you turn and face it. Naming the ghost is facing it. It will help you to identify the intensity of your reactions, but you are going to go deeper in this process. Now, ask yourself a few more questions:

How are my circumstances different now from how they were when the ghost was in my life?

_____

_____

_____

It is probable that at this stage of life you have more power and more choices than you did before. You might still be angry or hurt by a similar comment today, but gradually you will find you can say "I am angry" or "I am hurt," and the power of the comments will stop. You probably did not have as much personal power when you were with the "ghost." Now, ask yourself:

◊ *What is it about my partner that reminds me of the ghost?*
◊ *In what ways are they similar to one another?*
◊ *Do they look like each other?*
◊ *Does my partner have similar mannerisms?*
◊ *Do they like similar foods?*

List anything at all that makes them alike:

_____
_____
_____

Get rid of that ghost!

Ask yourself a few more questions. You have identified how your partner and the ghost are alike, and you've looked at what it is about the situations that seem similar. If any other comparisons come to mind as you work on this, add them to the list. Often, very small qualities—even the way someone blinks—can trigger a ghost response; so, take your time and be thorough about this list.

You've also asked yourself to look at how your circumstances have changed since that earlier time and how you now have more power and choice than you might have had then.

Week
13

◊ *What changes and growth do you see in yourself since the "ghost" was part of your life?*

List some of them:

_____

_____

_____

_____

Now focus on unlocking the connection between your partner and the ghost. Instead of similarities you are now going to look at differences. Again, be as specific as you can be and include as many details as you can in your list. Observe the following categories:

- Physical: height, weight, hair color, eye color.
- Ways of relating: talking, voice quality, listening, attentiveness.
- Mannerisms: sitting, walking, interacting with others, laughing, crying, working.

◊ *What are the ways in which your partner is different from the ghost?*

List all the differences which you can see in your partner and begin to focus on them.

_____

_____

_____

_____

Train yourself to banish the ghost by focusing on your partner, that person who is with you NOW! If there are physical differences start to focus on them immediately. They are the easiest to see.

 Ready to go on? Chris and Pat are going to help us out again.

Pause here and help Pat and Chris deal with their ghosts and the influence those ghosts have on the tensions between them about money:

Pat had attended a private school and had been raised in a household in which money was never a real concern. Pat's mother, Katie, however, never seemed to adjust to the family's wealth. She insisted on saving coins in an old mayonnaise jar in the kitchen and counted out those coins for Pat's allowance; and she was always questioning the need to pay for different school events and projects.

On the other hand, Chris did well in the public schools, was elected to Student Council and played basketball; but at home money was tight. When field trips and overnight athletic events happened, they had to be discussed thoroughly and planned for in advance. In spite of this reality, Chris's dad, Nick, wore the best quality suits, replaced the family car every three years and was always the person who picked up the check for restaurant bills. He believed in spending generously and lavishly, whether the mortgage had been paid that month or not.

As adults, Pat and Chris have been together for almost thirty years. They have watched their kids go to college. They've paid off the mortgage on their home, and it is time to talk about how they want this "empty nest" phase of life to play out.

Chris thinks it is important to keep working and is still very conservative about the family budget. Pat thinks the "nest egg" for the "empty nest period" is pretty large and would like to travel and see the world now that they no longer have financial responsibility for the kids. From Chris's point of view this is an extravagant and possibly irresponsible step to take.

Week 13

Here is how the ghost phenomenon works in this case: Whenever Pat hears Chris express concerns about the budget, *Katie's* voice comes through instead, and Pat experiences frustration and anger rather than being able to have a real conversation with Chris about *their* situation.

When Pat expresses this frustration and talks about wanting to spend money and travel, Chris hears *Nick* and becomes frightened that they may get into real financial problems if Pat's ideas are followed. They need to talk. Help them out.

Deal with their ghosts by helping them each identify the probable messages they received about money in their childhood.

Pat's messages from the "ghosts" of the past:

_____

_____

_____

_____

Pretend you knew Katie when Pat was young. Describe what she was like.

_____

_____

_____

_____

Chris's messages from the "ghosts" of the past:

_____

_____

_____

_____

Pretend you knew Nick when Chris was young. Describe what he was like.

_____

_____

_____

_____

Clearly state Pat's issue(s).

_____

_____

_____

_____

Clearly state Chris's issue(s).

_____

_____

_____

_____

If you want some extra practice working with processing, you could use this example and work your way through the steps as you did earlier in the book, but the main focus for you right now is to look at your own lives. **If ghosts are active in your relationship, use the worksheet on the following pages to help yourselves banish them.** If you are not bothered by ghosts, skip the worksheet and continue reading the chapter. The next section is about how early family experiences can lead to impasse triggers.

Week
13

Worksheet for Banishing Ghosts

Name that ghost:

List some of the ghosts you think you may have brought with you to this relationship:
*1)*_____
*2)*_____
*3)*_____

Pick one. If you know which ghost triggers you to have a strong reaction with your partner, pick that one: _____.

Name that ghost: I believe I have brought _____into this relationship.

Take some time to remember the circumstances of the period of time when this ghost was powerful in your life. Look at the questions above (p. 134) to get some ideas.

LIST some of the ways in which you have changed since the time this person was in your life:
*1)*_____
*2)*_____
*3)*_____

It is probable that you are a stronger, more independent and more secure-in-yourself person now than you were then. Even if you are not able to see those qualities yet, you are—at the very least—older. These differences are important because awareness of them helps you to stay in the present. You want to be solidly in your own skin if you are dealing with a ghost. What makes the ghost powerful is that something about your partner triggers that old response in you and part of you slides back into those long-ago times.

Week 14

List some similarities between your partner and the ghost:

1)_____

2)_____

3)_____

Now let's get rid of that ghost:

List as many things about your partner as you can that are different from the ghost:

1)_____

2)_____

3)_____

Pick the most striking physical difference between your partner and the ghost and focus on that. It may be his eyes, her arms, his weight, her height. Focus on the difference. Write here what you think the most striking physical difference is:

_____

_____

_____

Remind yourself that this is who you are with now and practice looking at this aspect of your partner from time to time. The next time you start to feel influenced by the "ghost", focus on your partner's eyes or arms or smile. Breathe. Remember where you are and who this person is. When you do this, the ghost has no power.

Before going ahead, spend some time talking with one another about this particular ghost and begin to brainstorm how your lives with one another might improve without this "ghost" around. Pause before moving on to the next exercise. Go get a cup of tea, take a walk, take a hot bath, hit some tennis balls. Take a break.

Week 14

How are you doing with the daily talks and weekly meetings? If you are using the motivational envelope, stop and tally the total and see how much money you have.

Keep going after your break, but stop and congratulate yourselves!

Part Two - Family Influences

The place to look for family influences is in what is called your family of origin—basically the family you grew up in. If you grew up with your grandmother acting as your mother, that would be the household to look at. If your parents were divorced and each one remarried, you have three or even four households to examine: the original household with both your parents in it, your subsequent living situation and finally the households of each of your parents with their new spouses. This can get complicated. If you were lucky enough to have grown up in the household with your two original parents, your quest for finding the influences will be simpler—not necessarily yielding happier pictures, but at least simpler.

What you are looking for here are strong messages you received about how life "should" be led. As a couple you are looking further for distinct differences in these messages. On the surface, what may look like clear differences may not be that at all. My husband was raised as an Orthodox Jew. I was reared in a strict Irish Catholic home. You would think our family messages would be vastly different, but as we have compared notes over the years, we have discovered that the values taught in the two different home settings were far more similar than different.

Week 14

Even with those similarities, there were stylistic differences, patterns of living and behaving that differed in our two families.

For instance, my family of origin was much more verbal, and we were raised to be punsters. We did this because it was fun, though also as a way of interacting with our dad, who did not relate well emotionally—lived in his head—but had a quick wit. Such humor can add a great richness to life, but it also provides a place to hide. Humor can deflect intimacy very quickly.

Bernie's family taught that staying busy and being productive were important. Again, these are fine attributes, and they became essential after his father died when he was nine years old. These attributes allowed him to succeed in school and later in his profession, yet it was possible to get lost in the "to-dos" of existence and miss the opportunities for simple fun. Each influence—humor, productivity—can be both positive and negative. As a couple the challenge is to see how these different influences we bring to the relationship enhance or diminish intimacy between us.

Toxic Messages

Some early family messages are toxic. These messages are so strong that they have already inhibited your development. Toxic messages come from abusive situations. They also come from situations in which the rules for living are so tight that there is no room for safe experimentation as you grow up. If you look at your family messages and realize that they were toxic, treat yourself to some therapy sessions and examine those messages. Just because you have carried them this far does not mean that you need to keep carrying them.

Changing Toxic Messages

Week
14

If you have identified messages you received as a child which you think might have been "toxic" or, at the very least, are interfering with your life in the present, list one of them here:

_____

_____

Now, look at the message and state it in one clear sentence:

_____

_____

We will return to this sentence shortly.

 Remember Judy and David, one of the couples from the Introduction? They are going to help us out in this section on family influences.

One of Judy's early messages from her dad was: "Always listen to your mother." A truck driver, he would say this as he left on a three-day run. It was his way of supporting his wife from a distance, but Judy internalized that message, and in her brain it became much more strict than he had ever intended. In her mind the sentence she still has is, "Always do everything your mother wants you to do." This last year that sentence has added stress for her because it presented such an impossible standard. With three children, she just couldn't always do what her mother wanted or even what she felt her mother needed. Judy needs to update this sentence inside her head and change it to something more manageable.

We'll walk through this technique with her, and then you can try it with your own sentence:

First, Judy sits quietly and either closes her eyes or looks at the ground. This technique is a little bit like meditating. Sitting calmly, she pays attention to her breathing for just a couple of minutes.

Second, after she feels calm and quieted she pictures in her mind that she is walking down a hallway. She opens one of the doors and finds a small room with a chalkboard on the far wall. The room reminds her a little of the children's Sunday School classroom.

Third, she looks at the chalkboard and sees that it has her sentence written on it:

> ### ALWAYS DO EVERYTHING YOUR MOTHER WANTS YOU TO DO

She looks at this for a few seconds and then she picks up the eraser and chalk and begins to change the sentence. She comes up with this revision:

> ### DO WHAT IS POSSIBLE FOR YOUR MOTHER AND TAKE CARE OF YOURSELF, TOO

She looks at this new sentence and says it a few times, resolving to keep this with her. In her mind's eye she walks out of the chalkboard room and quietly returns to paying attention to her breathing. She opens her eyes and says the new sentence aloud:

"Do what is possible for your mother and take care of yourself, too." She sighs with relief. This is a message she can use well at this time of her life.

Now it is your turn:

1) Sit quietly and either close your eyes or gaze peacefully at something around you. Pay attention to your breathing and let yourself become calm.

Week 14

2) Picture yourself walking down a hallway. Select one of the doors and open it.

3) See the chalkboard. On the board is YOUR sentence. Look at it clearly.

4) Pick up the eraser and chalk and work with that sentence. Erase it completely or change it around. Make it a sentence you know you can live with at this stage of your life.

5) Write the new sentence on the chalkboard and look at it. Resolve to remember it.

6) In your mind's eye, walk out of that room, bringing your new sentence with you and return your focus to your own calm and quiet breathing. Open your eyes. Say your new sentence out loud or to yourself. Write it down. Look at it. Let it sink into you. Sigh with relief or excitement and think about how this new sentence might help you change how you live your life every single day.

Other Messages

Most messages are not toxic. Some are just plain silly, but they are presented with such seriousness that they feel like true rules for life and get treated with that level of respect and restrictiveness. I had a funny experience after I left the convent. For the first six months or so I found myself periodically living with two different families. These were wonderful settings for me to transition from having been a nun to becoming a regular woman, and both families contributed tremendously to my life. Living in each of those little communities, however, brought some funny moments.

Week
14

? Salad-Making Rules ?

I was helping out in the kitchen of the first family early on in my stay there. We were fixing dinner, and my job was the salad. I took out the head of lettuce and began tearing off large pieces of greens for the salad bowl.

"Oh no," I was told, "that's not how you prepare greens for a salad."

Well, it was the way my mother had taught me, and it worked well enough in my family so I was a bit surprised by the intensity of the rebuke. "Okay," I said, "how do you want it done?"

"This is how it is done. You cut the greens into small slices and put them in the bowl."

Well, I could do that, and I knew this wasn't the time to discuss the history of how I learned to build a salad, but I chuckled that this was "the way" to do it.

About a month later, I was in the household of the second family, again given the job of preparing the salad. I took the greens and began cutting them as I had been shown in the first household.

"Oh no," I was told, "that's not how you prepare greens for a salad."

A little déjà vued here, I quickly said, "How would you like the greens prepared?"

"This is the way you fix greens for a salad. You tear them—but in small bite-sized pieces—and put them in the bowl."

These incidents occurred over thirty five years ago but if you invited me into your home today and asked me to help with the salad, I'd start the process by asking you how you wanted the greens prepared!

Week 14

It is a funny illustration of how "ways of doing things" can become "rules for how things should be done." Obviously, there are lots of ways to prepare a salad as there are lots of ways to do a lot of things. There really is not only one way to do the laundry, for instance, or to vacuum a room or to organize a closet. There are lots of ways to do these things, and as a couple living together, your job is to figure out which of these styles works best for both of you. These are not moral issues. Really, they are not.

☯ Help Judy and David identify family influences:

It sometimes surprises us to see how early family influences still linger in ways we might not have considered. These influences are more powerful for Judy and David now, because of the recent death of Judy's dad. Grief makes them each more vulnerable. On the surface the content you are about to read is about compliments and work stresses, but it is also about the early influences of Judy's family on her responses. Read what is happening between them and help them out of this situation.

Judy has been bothered for a long time by the way David does not notice when she has put a lot of effort into looking nice for an evening out. His lack of comment makes her feel ugly and old, and she finds herself getting suspicious that David is no longer interested in her and might even be seeing another woman. In addition, she has memories from her family growing up of her mother going into the bedroom and crying after her father said something loud and critical to her. Judy always felt sorry for her mom and angry at her father about this. When David ignores her, he reminds her of her dad's coldness and his critical nature, and this makes her hurt and angry.

Judy doesn't yet know that David has been under pressure at work to accept a promotion that would involve the two of them doing a lot of socializing. Although the extra money would be good, he

Week
14

always feels a certain edge around Judy whenever they go out, and he doesn't think she could endure much more socializing.

Before this builds further and Judy and David become more distanced from each other, let's help them go through the steps and deal with this situation:

Let's say that David decides to bring up his hesitancy about accepting the new job position:

1) How would you suggest that he present his issue?

_____

_____

_____

2) What specific change might he ask for?

_____

_____

_____

3) Put that request into "I" language for him:

_____

_____

_____

4) Knowing what you do about this issue from Judy's point of view, list the possible barriers she will have to hearing this issue clearly:

_____

_____

_____

Week 14

These are the reactions and issues that Judy must put aside in order to hear David's request.

Assuming she has found a way not to get distracted, help her give a response to David's request.

"It is hard for me to hear your request because so many of my own issues get triggered, but I am working to pay attention to what you are asking. Here is what I am willing to do:

_____

_____

_____

Does that help?"

David: "Yes, thank you. That's a good start."

There are no right or wrong answers to the above. The main challenge for David is to express his concerns clearly and simply, and the main challenge for Judy is to hear the request without getting caught up in her own related and very legitimate issues.

Now, go back and switch things around. Take the same situation from Judy's point of view and have her ask for what she wants. Her issue is simple on the surface but because it is tied to so many past emotions, she could use some help in distinguishing between her current real issue with David and the issues she has with the "ghosts" of her parents and some of their messages to her.

1) How would you suggest to her that she begin to figure out who the ghosts are and how to free herself from them?

_____

_____

_____

2) Let's assume she's taken the steps you suggested and has more understanding of herself around this issue. Now she is ready to tell David what she wants. Give her some ideas about how to phrase her issue:

_____

_____

_____

3) What is a specific change she might ask for from David?

_____

_____

_____

4) What might make it difficult for David to hear this clearly?

_____

_____

_____

5) How would you suggest he begin to distinguish between his own reactions and what is actually being asked here?

_____

_____

_____

6) Once he has followed your advice and gotten to the place where he is ready to respond, give him some suggestions about what he might offer in response.

_____

_____

_____

Now that you have helped David and Judy do this, it is time to look at your own family influences. Plan to do this at your next weekly meeting.

Week
14

Consider this . . .

Anne's Reflections

<u>It is time to forgive.</u> It is such an easy pattern to fall into—holding on to hurts and angers over the years and sometimes over the decades. Some of the times, the trigger for our emotion has been a harsh and cruel incident. Sometimes it has resulted from insults over a period of time. Sometimes it originated from our misinterpretation of a situation. Sometimes we have been used by others who seem to have more power than we do.

The problem for us is that as long as we hold onto the pain or the hurt or the anger of these incidents, we are the ones who are paying the price. The reason for forgiveness, from an emotional perspective, is to give up the burden we have been carrying. Period. We benefit. Once we can see clearly what we have been carrying, it is time to forgive.

12

WRAPPING UP AND MOVING ON

In reading this book and working the different exercises, you have learned that the key to a fluid and alive intimate life is the ability to be with and hear one another, even in the hard times.

This happens only when you set aside the time to be together, the time to enjoy one another and the time to work out any differences that come up between you. You have established those times and made yourselves your own priority. You have put aside twenty minutes a day to simply catch up with one another. You have scheduled and kept a one-hour-a-week "business" meeting about your relationship and you are devoting at least two hours a week to simply having fun—together. Congratulations!

You also now know a set of processing "Steps" to follow to help you with working out any differences. You've followed our versatile couple, Chris and Pat, through many situations. You've helped them out of a few!

Week 14

If you get stuck with one another around some issue—really stuck—you now know that simply means that, for a variety of reasons, you have stumbled into an impasse. The key to getting out of the impasse is finding the 1% solution—the 1% place of connection or agreement which puts you back in the game again. In addition to knowing there is the possibility of finding this 1%, you know some specific skills to use to get there.

You have learned to speak "in longhand." You have practiced "brainstorming to the absurd." You know how to switch sides and "take the other person's point of view." The two of you have established "rituals" which you agree to follow no matter how estranged or angry you might feel toward one another; and you have experienced the connection that those rituals help you to maintain. You have also learned how to "translate" one another's language when necessary. You have learned these skills, and now they are yours. You can use them, adapt them, change them, throw them out. They are yours.

Together we've discussed impasse triggers such as the power of "ghosts" from the past and the ongoing influence of those early years in your family. We have also talked about the "Infamous Six"—the six topics that almost every couple has to deal with: sex, money, in-laws, children, household tasks and time. You now have an understanding that you are not alone when you are in the midst of a situation involving one of those topics. You can stay calm, stay together and apply "The Steps" to work out strategies for each of them.

As I said in the Introduction, this book is for you. Keep it, refer to it, write in the margins, bend back pages, copy what you need. Use it!

This book can be a reference point for you in the future. The time you have set aside for your weekly meetings can be used for processing current issues, but it also can be used for anticipating changes or situations for you or your family. Maybe the children are approaching adolescence. If they are already eleven or twelve, it is time for the two of you to begin to prepare for how you are going to handle the next several years. Your weekly meeting is a good time for such conversations. Perhaps you are within a few years of retirement, or ready to sell a house or needing to get out of your job. Your weekly meeting is a place where any of these situations may be talked about. You have established a ritual for talking about all kinds of situations which affect your relationship. Use it creatively.

As you have been using this book and working on all of these exercises together, and as you've established the routine of setting aside time to process your own issues with one another, I hope an important, though subtle, change has happened in your relationship. I hope you feel the firmness of your commitment to one another differently than you did before. I hope you can feel that a foundation is being built with every issue you resolve and that you feel a confidence within you that you can work out anything.

That confidence is no longer just an assurance of your own individual strength. It is a confidence in yourselves as a couple. You begin to realize that between you, you have a strength, an endurance and a flexibility that you never would have imagined. The personhood of your relationship is developing its own selfhood separate from either of you. As you start to feel that happening, you will know you are on the right track.

Life dishes out all kinds of things to us. Some of them are delightful and some of them are frustrating and scary, but as this foundation strengthens, you realize that the two of you can handle it all—not necessarily gracefully, but competently. Other people will sense that change in you too, because you will engage with life as a couple with a quiet difference that they will be able to feel.

Week
14

I would like to close with a quotation from a Jewish mystic, the Baal Shem Tov. My sister and her husband gave us a print of the quote as a gift early in our marriage. Bernie and I have always treasured these words and their message inspired the title of this book.

You read the words at the beginning of this book, but pause and read them again because in the interim you have temporarily focused your lights inward, between yourselves, in order to make changes you felt were necessary. Now it is time to consider the power of your merged streams of light. This is what the Baal Shem Tov said:

> *From every human being there arises a light*
> *That reaches straight to heaven*
> *And when two souls that are destined to be together*
> *Find each other,*
> *Their streams of light flow together,*
> *And a single brighter light*
> *Goes forth from their united being.*

I offer my congratulations to you two for sticking with the process of reading and working on this book together, and, agreeing with the Baal Shem Tov, I say, "Let your light shine!"

Week
14

About the Author

Anne Burns Harris has worked as a psychologist in North Carolina since 1975. She and her husband, Bernie, and their chocolate Lab, Shayna, currently divide their time between Asheville, North Carolina, and Myrtle Beach, South Carolina. Each community feels like home, and they are privileged to be able to to enjoy the rich balance of mountain vistas and moonlight reflections playing on the sea.

www.anneburnsharris.com